A CONTEMPORARY LOOK AT SIKH RELIGION

A CONTEMPORARY LOOK AT SIKH RELIGION

Essays on Scripture, Identity, Creation, Spirituality, Charity and Interfaith Dialogue

JAMES MASSEY

CENTRE FOR DALIT/SUBALTERN STUDIES

MANOHAR
2010

First published 2010

ISBN 978-81-7304-857-9

Published by
Ajay Kumar Jain *for*
Manohar Publishers & Distributors
4753/23 Ansari Road, Daryaganj,
New Delhi 110 002

Printed at
Salasar Imaging Systems
Delhi 110 035

To my loving grandchildren

Ashreya Cherian, Zara Cherian
Azan Cherian, Zada Cherian

Contents

Preface

It was in October 1985, when I was invited to deliver a lecture on the theme 'Fresh Look at Sikh Religion' by the Faculty of Theology of the Johann Wolfgang Goethe-University, Frankfurt, Germany. This lecture not only received a very positive response from the faculty members, it also had an equally good response from Sikh readers, when it got published in the April 1987 issue of the *Journal of the Guru Nanak Foundation*, New Delhi. This was the beginning of my becoming a serious student of Sikh religion, which actually followed my doctoral thesis at the above-mentioned university on the subject 'The Doctrine of the Ultimate Reality in Guru Nanak's Hymns Found in the Standard Text of the Adi Granth'. After the acceptance of this work for my doctoral degree, it was subsequently published in 1991 (revised edition 2010) by Manohar Publishers, New Delhi. Following this, the further study of Sikh religion became part of my life in different levels. I have been asked time and again to contribute to write for Sikh and other journals as well as reviews. I have also been invited to make presentations at local, national and international level seminars organized by different academic bodies on the subject. The ten essays included in this work are the outcome of the same process. These essays were written at different times for different occasions, but for this work these have been revised and re-written keeping in view the needs of the present societal context of India as well as the world. The author believes that the message of the Sikh Gurus and other saints, found in the *Sri Guru Granth Sahibji*, which is the core of Sikh faith, is fully relevant in our time, as it was relevant at the time, when it was written.

Before I go on to elaborate about the content of the essays contains in this book, one question, I have to answer is the one my Sikh friends as well as others including Christians ask me often: How and why I became interested in such a serious study of Sikh faith particularly as a Christian? It is true that I am not only a Christian, but a fully committed Christian. But my answer to the question always includes my being a Punjabi Christian, who is very proud to be a Punjabi. But I am an Indian as well, of which also I am equally proud. The answer to the above question is actually hidden among these identities, which I am carrying in my being, because as I stand today, I have become fully aware of my identities, which actually have contributed to my 'thinking' or what we call 'ideology' or 'theology' of life. Among these identities, one is very special—that of my being a 'Punjabi'. As a Punjabi, the Punjabi culture which includes the Punjabi language are two factors which lies at the core of my Punjabi identity. One factor which influenced the formation of such an identity is the religious tradition, particularly for 'cultural heritage'. But we must remember that culture is not identical with religion, but it only draws some elements from a religion.

This is the reason why it is said that there is a very 'thin' line between religion and culture, but it is actually the cultural elements which keeps us together. But at the same time, unconscious to us, we continue to share those religious elements which got adopted as part of our culture, and it is those religious elements, which become common to all those who share that 'common identity'. In the case of 'Punjabi' or 'Punjabiat' as an identity, it certainly carries in it the 'values' of Sikh religion, because it has been a religion of the majority of inhabitants in Punjab for more than 500 years. It is these Punjabi cultural inherited Sikh values, which I carry in my being. I must add here, that I became more and more conscious of my 'Punjabi identity' from the mid-1970s onwards, which influenced my being as a Christian, the reflections of which can be seen in my book, *Christianity: An Introduction* (in Punjabi), which I wrote in 1976 and which is supposed to be written in 'Punjabi thought form', clearly seen rooted in the 'Sikh religious traditions' and which can be seen as the contribution of 'Sikh religion' to the 'Punjabi culture' or 'Punjabi Christianity'. My becoming more and more conscious of my Punjabi identity is the factor which is responsible for myself getting more and more drawn to the Sikh religion. This factor also made me richer as a Punjabi Christian. Seeing myself as part of the 'Punjabi Dalit Community' is another factor which helped me to see with such eyes 'Sikh faith' as well as 'Christian faith', if these offer any message or bring hope to this community (among whom Guru Nanak Devji placed himself as *neech* when he said, 'the lowest among the low-caste (*neech*)' (*SGGS*, p. 15). It is through the eyes of such people that attempt has been made to Look at the Sikh faith and also justifies the 'A Contemporary Look', which is part of the title of this volume.

The ten essays in this volume have been divided into four parts. In part one, the first essay deals with the Sikh Scripture, which includes *Sri Guru Granth Sahib*, containing the writings of 36 authors including the six Gurus. These authors, not only belonged to different regions of India, but even among them five came from the so-called 'out-castes' or 'untouchable' communities. The second essay in this part discusses in detail, the vision and mission of Universal Humanhood of Sri Guru Gobind Singhji. In part two, the two essays deal with 'Sikh identity', and shows that till today the struggle for identity is continuing. Part three contains four essays dealing with the Sikh concepts of 'creation', 'spirituality', 'charity' and 'suffering and death'. Part four contains two essays, one dealing with 'interfaith dialogue' offered by Sri Guru Nanak Devji and another, the last essay on the historical development of the same process, with special reference to the contribution of the Sikh community. The discussion of part four is offered with a belief that the 'interfaith dialogue' can become the most effective instrument to deal with the religious- and cultural-based troubled conditions prevailing in almost every human society, be it our own country India or the rest of the world.

This work is the result of the encouragement and help from many individuals and organizations to whom I would like to express my gratitude. I am specially thankful to the Centre for Dalit/Subaltern Studies, New Delhi for sponsoring the publication as part of its programme. I am specially thankful to my colleagues Chitaranjan Nag and Imti Jamir, who have helped in putting and arranging the materials very carefully through its many stages. I am indebted to my publisher Ramesh Jain and his son Ajay Jain for their valuable suggestions and keen interest in this publication. I am also grateful to my family members, specially my wife Kala, for patiently bearing with me during my pre-occupations while working on the essays included in this work.

Above all I am thankful to God Almighty for giving me the strength to complete this work, which I believe will provide the necessary support to people of different faiths and ideologies.

30 September 2009 JAMES MASSEY

Part One

SCRIPTURE

1

Sri Guru Granth Sahib: Ecumenical with a Holistic Message

1. INTRODUCTORY REMARKS

The discussion in this chapter is centred around the Sikh scripture, namely the *Sri Guru Granth Sahib*. The discussion will be limited to the two main aspects namely the 'ecumenical aspect' and the 'holistic message' of this holy book. But before that I would like to make a brief reference to the context of the time when the message was received by the Gurus and their various Bhagats, which today is part of this holy book.

2. THE CONTEXT

Guru Nanak Devji in *Var Majh Ki*, in one of the *dohas* (verse), gave a very clear visible overview of the context of his time as follows:

Kali katī raje kasāī dharamu pankh kari udariā.
Kūṛu amāvas sachu chandrmā dīsai nahi kāhā cṛiā.
Hau bhali vikuanī hoī.
Ādherai rāhu na koī.
Vici humai kari dukhu roī.
Kahu Nānak kini bidi gati hoī.

Kali-yuga is turned knife, rulers butchers;
Righteousness on wings is flown.
This is the dark night of evil;
The moon of truth is nowhere visible, nor risen.
For light have I searched to distraction—
No path in this darkness is visible.
Humanity in egoism involved, in suffering wails.
This Nanak seeks to know: How may liberation then be found?[1]

Bhai Gurdas, whose *vars* (writings) are considered as the key (*kunji*) to understand the *Sri Guru Granth Sahib*, has summed up the conditions previously before the birth of Guru Nanak Devji as follows:

Masters, the Dark Age is the vomit of dog which feeds on the flesh of corpses.
Kings commit sinful deeds and fences consume the crops they are meant to protect.
The people have become blind; devoid of understanding they utter evil and falsehood.
It is disciples who play the music, brothers and the guru
who in so many ways dance (to their tune).
Servants remain at ease in their homes while the master arises and goes to their houses.
The qazis have become corrupt, taking bribes and ignoring the rights (of the people)
Women's love for men is only money, regardless of its source.
Sin prevails throughout the entire world.[2]

Bhai Gurdas' *vars* are the commentary on the text of *Sri Guru Granth Sahib*, therefore this verse of his *var* is self-explanatory. So we will move to the discussion on 'ecumenical aspect'.

3. ECUMENICAL ASPECTS

Sri Guru Granth Sahib presents in a real sense the ecumenical spirit in its content, because among the 36 authors are included six Gurus, 15 Bhagats (Hindus and Muslims saints), 11 Bhats (all Hindu Brahmin musicians) and four others (three Muslims and one Hindu).[3] The authors, particularly the Bhagats came not only from different regional backgrounds, but they also belonged to different castes: five of them even belonged to the so-called 'lower castes'. This added to the richness of the ecumenical spirit of this Holy Book. Dr C.H. Loehlin describes the principles that Guru Arjan Devji used in the selection of the various writings that are included in the *Sri Guru Granth Sahib*: 'It is said that Guru rejected hymns of self-deification; those derogatory to women; those which advised the concealing of God's message from men; and those disparaging life and its struggles.'[4] The quotes given in the later discussion will show how these principles became operative in the text. As we will be referring to the hymns of the Gurus and of those authors who were considered untouchables later, I shall like to give here two examples, one from a Hindu Bhagat and one from a Muslim one, to elucidate this point.

Two hymns of Bhagat Jaidev (CE 1201-45) are included in the text of *Sri Guru Granth Sahib*. Jaidev, a Hindu Brahmin, who in one of his hymns while condemning wealth and beauty, lays stress on the contemplation of the Lord. He says:

Rāmu simaru pachutāhigā mana.
Pāpī jīarā lobhu karatu hai āju kāli uṭhi jāhigā.
Lālaca lāge janamu gavāīā bharam bhulāhigā.
Dhana jobana kā garabu na kījai kāgada jiu gali jāhigā.
Jau jamu āi kesa gahi patakai tā kina kchu na basāhiga.
Simaranu bhajanu daiā nahī kīnī tau mukhi coṭā khāhigā.

My self! contemplate the Lord, else shall thou in regrets have to fall,
My sinful self, given avarice!
know, in a day or two shalt thou depart.
In attachment to greed lost thou wasted thy life,
And by *Maya*—illusion deluded.
Be not proud of wealth and beauty:
Know, like a piece of paper shall thou turn pulp.
The day that *Yama*, grasping thee by the heir, overthrows thee,
Powerless shall thou be.
As in contemplation, devotional chant, compassion hast thou not been engaged,
On thy face shalt receive buffets.[5]

The hymns of Baba Farid (CE 1175-1265), who was a Muslim by faith (Qureshi), are also included along with the writings of other Bhagats. Few of his *dohas* (verses) are given here as examples, in which he lays emphasis on forgiveness as a virtue and looks to the Lord for help. He says:

Pharīdū jo toi mārni mukīān tinhan na māre ghunmi.
Aāpanaṛai ghara jāīai pāira tinān di cumin.
Phārdā jān tau khataṇ vel tan tū ratā dunī siu.
Mārag svāī nīhi jan bhariā tan ladiā.
Dekhu pharīdū jo thīā dāṛī hoī bhūra
Agahu neṛā āiā picha rahia duri.
Dekhu pharidū ji thīā sakara hoī visu.
Sanī bājhhu apani vedaṇ kahīai kisu.

Farid, strike not back those strike thee blow;
In utter humanity and forgiveness turn towards thy home.
Farid ! time when thou couldst garner merit, wast
thou engrossed in the world.
Now with death's foundation firmly laid must thou depart,
When thy sack is loaded.
Look, Farid! what has befallen thee:
Thy beard turned grey,
Thy end approaching, the past far behind.
Look, Farid! What has come to pass:
Life sweet as sugar is turned to bitter poison.
To whom to relate my tale of sorrow but the Lord?[6]

4. HOLISTIC MESSAGE

It must be categorically emphasized that it is the holistic message of *Sri Guru Granth Sahib*, which gives to this Holy Book its rare uniqueness. If one carefully goes through the content of the hymns in it, one will find that it covers all aspects of human life including man's relationship with God, the Ultimate Reality, and the salvation or liberation of human beings. The authors of *Sri Guru Granth Sahib* have dealt with the basic contextual issues of their times by specially questioning the atrocities committed by the tyrannical rule of the Mughals, the evils of the caste system and the status of women. While addressing these and other issues in their prophetic messages, the Gurus and Bhagats made a complete paradigm shift. Given below are a few examples to illustrate this point.

4.1 *Creedal Statement*

During Guru Nanak Devji's time many different views about the nature of God were in existence. Keeping in mind all the prevailing views and definitions, in the opening book of *Sri Guru Granth Sahib*, Guruji made a basic statement of his faith, which later became the fundamental creedal statement for the Sikhs known as *Mul Mantr*, which reads as follows:

Ik Oṁkār Satināmu Karta purakhu Nirbhau
Nirvīru Akāl-mūrati Ajūni Saibhang Gurprasādī.

He is Sole Supreme Being; eternal manifestation;
Creators, Immanent Reality; Without Fear;
Without Rancour; timeless Form; Unincarnated;
Self-existent; Realized by grace of the holy Preceptor.

After stating this basic faith-statement about the nature of Ultimate Reality and how one attains the knowledge of the same, Guru Nanak Devji raised some other basic questions, but before that he summarized the existing prescribed ways to achieve salvation, as follows:

Ādī sacu Jugādi sacu
Hai bhi sacu
Nānak hosī bhī sacu
Socai soci na hovai je soci lakh vār.
Cupai cup na hovaī e lāī rahā liv tār.
Bhukhiā bhukh na utrī je bannā purīa bhār.
Sahas siānpā lakh hohi ta ik na calai nāli

In primal Time, is all Time, was the Creator;
Nothing is real but the Eternal.
Nothing shall last but the Eternal.
Ritual purification; though millions-fold,
May not purify the mind;
Nor may absorption in trance still it, however long and continuous.

Possessing worlds multiple quenches not the rage, avarice and desire.
A thousand million feats of intellect brings not emancipation.

In this way Guru Nanak Devji has reflected on all the possible traditional methods or ways to solve or answer the basic question of human quest, which he stated as follows:

Kiv saciārā hoīai kiv kuṛai tutai pāli

How then to become true to the Creator?
How to demolish the wall of illusion?

Guruji's own answer to this is:

Hukami rajāi calṇā Nānaka likhiā nalī

Through Obedience to His Ordinance and Will.[7]

Guru Nanak Devji further in *Japu Sahib* discusses different aspects of the same question, but his firm conviction was that it is only through the grace of God that one can get salvation. He states:

Karmī āvai kapṛā nadarī mokhu duāru

By man's actions is acquired the vesture of human incarnation;
By God's grace is attained the Door of liberation.[8]

4.2 *An Alternative Social Order*

All through the text of the *Granth Sahib*, social equality among human beings is upheld and it rejects completely caste-based distinctions, as well as rituals based on *karma* or deeds. For example, in *Japu Sahib*, Guru Nanak Devji had declared that before God all are equal:

Nānaka utamu nīchu na koe

Saith Nanak:
All before Him are alike—
None high or low.[9]

Guru Nanak Devji totally rejected caste exclusiveness and declared his complete solidarity with those considered outcastes (*neech*)—or today's Dalits—by declaring himself to be:

Nēcā andari nēca jāti nīcī hū ati nīcu.
Nānaku tin kai sangi sāthi vadiā siū kiā rīs.
Jithai nēca samālīani tithai nadir terī bakhsīs.

The lowest among the low-caste;
those still lower and condemned—
Nanak is by their side;
He envies not the great of the world.
Lord! Thy grace falls on the land,
Where the poor are cherished.[10]

Guru Amar Dasji while arguing against the caste system declares that false ideas behind the so-called certain castes only give rise to human pride, which is actually harmful for achieving the final life goal. Therefore Guru Amar Dasji strongly recommends:

Jāti kā garabu na krīahu.
Barhamu binde so brāhaman hoi.
Jāti kā garabu na kari mūrakha gavārā.
Isu garaba te calahi bahutu vikārā.

Pride of caste let none entertain:
One realizing the Supreme Being is *alone* a Brahmin.
Thou ignorant fool, entertain not pride of caste!
By such pride manifold mischief arise.

Guru Amar Dasji again emphasizes this point by making it clear that all human beings are created from the same source. He says:

Cāre varan ākhai sabhu koi.
Barhamu bind te sabh opati hoi.
Mātī eka sagali sansārā.
Bahu bidhi bhānḍe ghṛai kumārā.
Panc tatu mili deh̤i kā ākārā.
Ghati vadhi ko karai bīcīrā.

All talk of the four castes:
Know that all creation from the Divine
Essence has arisen.
The whole universe from the same clay *has appeared*:
The Potter however, in numerous forms makes the vessels.

From five elements is made the form of the body—
Who may consider which has less of these or more.[11]

Sri Guru Granth Sahib rejects outright the castes-based social order and caste practices. Its compiler Guru Arjun Devji has even included in it the hymns composed by the so-called untouchable saints. This shows that in the eyes of the Gurus, outcastes, considered untouchables then, were not only welcome to receive religious ministrations, but they were also offered the pride of place of a teacher, which at that time was forbidden even to higher castes other than the Brahmins. Three such examples of untouchable (Dalits) saints are: Kabir, a weaver; Ravidas, a cobbler and Namdev, a dyer. Guru Arjan Devji believed that 'in each vessel does the Lord abide'.[12] Quotes from the hymns of Namdev and Kabir, based on their experiences are given below.

In the following hymn Namdev vehemently condemns the maltreatment given to him on his first visit to a Hindu temple. When the so-called upper caste devotees realized that he was a low caste washerman, they pushed him out of the temple. Pained by this treatment, he retired to the courtyard behind the temple and there he had an intimate experience with God, as a result of which the doors of the temple turned towards him. He narrated this experience thus:

Hasata khelata tere dehure āiā.
Bhagati karata nāmā pakare uthaiā.
Hīnar jāti merī jādama rāiā.
Chīpe ke janami kāhe ku āiā.
Lai Kamalī caleo palatāi.
Dehurai pāchai baithā jāi.
Jiu jo nāmā hari gun ucarai.
Bhagata janan kau dehura phirai.

In a cheerful mood to Thy temple I came,
While performing devotion, was *Nama* pushed off.
Lord of Yadava race! low is my caste.
Why didst thou give me birth in a dyer's home?
Picking up my woollen sheet, back I turned,
And sat in the temple's rear.
While *Nama* the Lord's laudation was uttering
The temple door towards the devotee turned.[13]

A low-caste Muslim saint, Kabir, has gone still further and attacked the so-called high caste Brahmins directly and asked them if they can prove that they are different from other human beings. He argued:

Garabh vāsa mahi kalu nahī jātī.
Barhama bindu te sabha ūtapātī.
Taū āna bāta kāhe nahī āiā.
Tuma kata barhamana hama kata sūda.
Hama kata lohū tuma kata dūdha.
Kahu Kabīra ho barhamu bīcārai.

In the lodgment in the womb exists neither family pride nor caste:
All beings from the Divine essence have created.
Say thou Pandit! when did Brahmins originate?
Do not make waste of thy human incarnation,
By boasting of thy Brahmin origin.
If thou doest claim to be a Brahmin by thy birth from a Brahmin woman,
Why was thy birth not from a different source?
How are you Brahmins and we Sudras?
How were we made of mere blood, and you of milk?
Saith Kabir: Among us is he alone known as Brahmin, who the Supreme Being contemplates.[14]

These are the few examples included in *Sri Guru Granth Sahib* about the issue of caste. Finally a quotation is given from one of Guru Nanak Devji's hymns, in which he has not only rejected the caste system as a whole which labels some as low caste or untouchable or outcaste, but he has also revealed who really are the 'the real untouchables'. Part of this hymn reads thus:

Kobodhi ḍūmaṇī kodaiā kasaiṇi para nindā
ghat cūhaṛī muṭhī korudli candali.
Kārī karī kiā thīai jān cāre baiṭhīa nail.
Sacu sanjam karaṇi kārān nūvṇu nāujapehī.
Nānaka agai ūtama seī ji pāpān pandi na dehī.

Evil-doing, hard-heartedness, slander, violence—
These are the real untouchables.
How is your cooking-space pure with these low-caste women beside you?
True ritual of purity is truthfulness;

Good actions your kitchen-bounds;
Prayer, true holy bath.
Saith Nanak: With God such only are considered noble,
As preach not to others sinful ritual.[15]

Thus, *Sri Guru Granth Sahib* not only completely rejects caste-based distinctions and practices, it also laid down the foundation of an alternative 'social order' based upon the principles of 'purity of truthfulness', 'good actions', and 'prayer'. Here we also see the basis of the three fundamental concepts, *kirt karo* ('work' with one's own hands), *nam japo* ('meditate' on the Divine name) and *vand chako* ('share' your food with others). In this way the authors of *Sri Guru Granth Sahib* (particularly the Gurus) did not only reflect on a caste-based 'social order', they in fact laid down the foundation of Sikh praxis, because it demanded actual action with the reflection.

4.3 *Paradigm Shift in Many Other Areas*

In *Sri Guru Granth Sahib*, the integrity and sacredness of the whole creation is fully upheld. This can be felt because of the very presence of the Creator in every created things of this world, and that includes the human beings as well. In this regard Guru Nanak Devji has said in *Var Asa*:

Āpīanai āpu sājio āpīnai racio nāum
Duyī kudarti sajīai kari āsanu diṭṭho cāu.

His self He created, and manifested His Name.
Then the second object, expanse of the universe He made;
Settled in His cushion, in joy He beheld it.[16]

Guru Nanak Devji as a prophet after seeing the upheaval created by Babur's invasion, challenged the Creator and even questioned Him by saying:

Khurāsāna Khasamānā kīā hindusatānu darāiā.
Āpai dosu na deī karatā jamu kari mugalu cṛāiā.
Etī mārā pai kuralāṇe tain kī daradu na āiā.

The Lord from Babur's invasion protected Khorasan,
And on Hindustan let loose the terror.

The Lord Himself punishes not:
So the Mughal Babur He sent down,
Dealing death as Yama.
As in their agony of suffering the people wailed,
Didst Thou feel no compassion for them?[17]

In a number of places, *Sri Guru Granth Sahib* reveals that even the religious leaders of different religions of Guruji's time have lost their integrity. Therefore, Guruji offered the alternative meaning of faith and asked everyone to follow these. For example, to the Hindu Brahmins he tells about the real holy thread (*janeu*), which they should wear always. Guruji says to them:

Daiā kapāha santokhu sūtu jatu gandhī sātū vatu.
Ehu janeū jiā kā haī ta pāḍe ghatu.

Make compassion the cotton, contentment the yarn;
Continence the knot and purity the twist;
Such is the true sacred thread of the self.
Thou Brahmin-priest! Put this on me shouldst thou have it.[18]

In another place, Guruji tells the Muslims the virtues of a true Muslim. He says:

Musalamanu kahāvanu musakalu jā hoi tā musalamaṇu kahavai.
Avali auli dīnu kari miṭhā masakala mānā malu musā ṇai.
Hoi musalamiu dīna muhāṇai maraṇu jivaṇa ka bharamu cukāvai.
Rab kī rajāi manne sira upari karatā manne āpu gavāvai.
Tu Nānaka saraba jīā miharanmati hoi ta musulamāṇu kahāvai.

Hard it is to deserve the name of Mussalman—
Only one truly so, may such be called.
First, must he hold in love the way of the holy;
Like iron on grindstone should he cast off his possessions.
In the way of the Preceptor should he have faith,
And banish illusion of death and life.
To the Lord's will should he be obedient:
With faith in the Creator as compassionate he becomes.
May he be called a Mussalman.[19]

The status of women is the other main concern in *Sri Guru Granth Sahib*. Because women were considered low, inferior and impure at that time, Guru Nanak Devji, while questioning this position of theirs in the society, bestowed upon them, the highest status by saying in *Var Asa*:

> *So kiu mandā ākahīā jitu janmahi rājāna.*
>
> Why revile her of whom are born great ones of the earth?[20]

About *Sutak*, according to which woman is considered impure for a number of days after childbirth, Guruji declares.

> *Mana kā sūtaku lobhu hai jihavā sūtaku kūṛu.*
> *Akhī sūtaku vekhaṇā paratia paradhana rūpu.*
> *Kannī sūtaku kani pai lāitabārī khāhi.*
> *Nānaka hansā ādamī bhadhe jama puri jāhi.*
>
> The mind's *sutak* is avarice, the tongue's falsehood;
> The eye's *sutak* coveting others' womenfolk's beauty and others' wealth.
> The ear's *sutak* is listening to slander.
> Saith Nanak: By such practices selves of human beings caught,
> To Yama's demesne in bonds are taken.[21]

Suttee was another evil practice of the time, according to which women were forced to jump into the funeral pyre of their husbands. Other Gurus too condemned this evil practice. Guru Amar Dasji while condemning it, gave a new meaning to the expression *suttee.* He said:

> *Sathīā ehi na ākhīani jo maṛiā lagi jalanni.*
> *Nānaka satīā jaṇīani ji birahe cota maran ni.*
> *Bh so satīā jaṇīani sīla santokhi rahanni*
> *Sevani sāī āpaṇā nita uthi sanmālanni.*
>
> These be not the true *suttees* who burns themselves in logs of wood,
> Saith Nanak: True *suttees* are those that bear the suffering of separation.
> These be the real *suttees* that abide in good conduct and contentment;
> Who served their Lord, and after ever cherish his memory.[22]

5. CONCLUDING REMARKS

In conclusion, it may be reiterated that *Sri Guru Granth Sahib* is not only a unique text that is ecumenical in nature, but above all it gives a 'holistic' universal message, because it offered on the one hand a holistic approach to the human life, and on other it is a meant for all times, including the present. Besides dealing with doctrinal clarity the issue of caste and its evils, it has dealt with other important issues as well, such as integrity of the whole creation, the status of women, *suttee,* etc. Education and awareness about these and other issues, related to women specially, need more attention today, because the ratio of women to men is fast dwindling in most of the developed states of India. The evil of female foeticide has increased too and the caste issue continues to challenge society: marriages are still taking place on basis of caste and so is our places of worship (including the Gurdwaras).

I conclude with a quotation from the English translation of a part of one of the stanzas of *Var* by Bhai Gurdas, who was also the first Sikh theologian:

> In the Dark Age (with its multitude of deities) he revealed that there is but one, the Supreme God.
> (He made firm) the bases of the four pillars of *dharma*, and the four *varnas* he created one.
> He regarded king and beggar as equal and caused the virtue of humility to be practised in the world.
> Behold the manner in which God reverses accepted orders, how he makes heads (which are held high) to bow to the feet!
> Baba (Nanak) redeemed the Dark Age by proclaiming the *mantra* of the True Name.
> Guru Nanak came for the redemption of the Dark Age![23]

NOTES

1. *Sri Guru Granth Sahib* (*SGGS*) (English translation of *Sri Guru Granth Sahib* by Gurbachan Singh Talib, Patiala used throughout this chapter), p. 145.
2. Ganda Singh (ed.), *The Panjab Past and Present* (parts I and II), Patiala, 1969, p. 36.
3. See for details in: Talib, *Sri Guru Granth Sahib* (English translation), vol. 1, Patiala, 1984, Introduction, p. xxxviii. Also see: C.H. Loehlin, *The Sikhs and Their Scriptures*, Lucknow, 1964, pp. 31-6.
4. Loehlin, ibid., p. 32.
5. *SGGS*, p. 1106.

6. Ibid., p. 1378.
7. Ibid., p. 1.
8. Ibid., p. 2.
9. Ibid., p. 7.
10. Ibid., p.15.
11. Ibid., p. 1128.
12. Ibid., p. 747.
13. Ibid., p. 1164.
14. Ibid., p. 324.
15. Ibid., p. 91 (see Introduction, vol. 1, p. xxxiii).
16. Ibid., p. 463.
17. Ibid., p. 360.
18. Ibid., p. 471.
19. Ibid., p. 141.
20. Ibid., p. 473.
21. Ibid., p. 472.
22. Ibid., p. 787.
23. Ganda Singh (ed.), op. cit., p. 33.

2

Vision of Universal Humanhood: Sri Guru Gobind Singh

1. INTRODUCTORY REMARKS

The discussion in this chapter centres around one basic theme, the 'Vision of Universal Humanhood in Sri Guru Gobind Singh's Teachings'. The structure and the method followed in the discussion in this chapter is simple. After a brief discussion on the context (political, religious and social) of Sri Guru Gobind Singhji's time in the next section, Guruji's vision and mission are stated in section three, followed by a discussion on the 'institution of Khalsa' as an instrument of establishing the 'Universal Humanhood' in section four. In the fifth section the continuing challenge of the Guruji to the *Sikh Sangat* and all those others who believe in the common 'humanity' is dealt with. The chapter closes with a brief 'concluding remarks'.

2. CONTEXT AT THE TIME OF GURUJI

Since a vision and mission is always linked with a human situation of a particular time, including the political, social and religious milieu, Guruji himself has offered to help to know about the situation that existed both before his birth as well as that prevailed in his lifetime. One of his most authentic compositions is *Bachitra Nataka* (lit. meaning the 'Wonderful Drama'), which contains his autobiographical details.[1] In *Bachitra Nataka* while giving his family tree, he gave a clear picture of the distorted conditions of society not only during his time, but also at the time of the birth of Guru Nanak Devji. About the religious situation, of the time, he wrote in one of the *Doharas,*

> The (so-called) Brahmins became full of low instincts and Kshatriyas became traders (of their valour). The traders on account of their wealth started considering themselves mighty (Kshatriyas) and the low instincted people engrossed in evil propensities became leaders of the religious affairs (earlier undertaken by Brahmins).[2]

We get from the *Bachitra Nataka* a clear picture of the extreme form of political persecution of Hindus, including their forced conversion to Islam from the hands of the religious fanatic Mughal Emperor Aurangzeb. A summary of the holy sacrifice and how Guruji's father, Sri Guru Tegh Bahadurji sacrificed his life for others is given in one of the *chaupais* (a form of poetry) in *Bachitra Nataka* where he says: 'The lord protected his glory and discipline (of serving the cause of others) and driven by this feeling he enacted a great holocaust in this dark age (*kaliyuga*). To protect the honour of the innocent he sacrificed (his life). He offered his head but never gave any expression of pain.'[3] This *chaupai* reveals to us the truth about the nature of Aurangzeb's atrocities against the Hindus and the way Sri Guru Tegh Bahadurji saved the Hindu faith and fought for the freedom of religion.

The author of *Sri Dasam Guru Chamatkar* (a biography), while describing the condition of India at the time of the tenth Guruji's birth, summed up the same for us in these words: 'Aurangzeb was a fanatic Muslim and to enhance his political and religious position, he could go to any extent against the Hindus, which in fact he was doing. For the Hindus his rule was the rule of injustice and most troublesome.'[4]

Besides the challenge of Emperor Aurangzeb's fanaticism, another challenge the Guruji faced was from the Sikh missionary order known as *masands* (representatives), which by that time had also become corrupt. After the death of Guru Tegh Bahadurji the *masands* were in favour of maintaining *status quo*. They went to *Mataji* (the honourable mother) and complained about Sri Guru Gobindji. They were not in favour of Guruji's giving martial training to the Sikhs and complained to *Mataji*,

> On one side Guruji is in opposition with Aurangzeb, and on the other side now we will have enmity with the Hill Rajas (Hindu hill kings); in that case from all sides the Sikh congregations will stop coming; then from where we will get fund to take care of the needs of these soldiers and horses?[5]

About the type of corruption, which had entered the lives of the *masands*, the author of *Sri Dasam Guru Chamatkar* narrates a story about a leading *masand*, Bulaki Das, and a *palki* (palanquin). This story goes back to the time when Guru Gobindji was still in Patna and was planning to go to the Punjab. Mata Nanakiji, under the influence of the *masands*, wanted Guruji to continue to stay in Patna. According to her, *masands* were able to take care of all their needs. Guruji tried explaining to *Mataji* that these *masands* had become corrupt, keeping most of the donations to the Sikh congregations with themselves and depositing only a small portion of it to the treasury of Guruji. To prove his point, Guruji sent a word to one of the leading *masands* Bulaki Das, to send Guruji a *palki* made of wood and 7,000 grams of gold. *Masand* Bulaki Das according to the Guruji's order made the *palki* and sent the same to Guruji. After receiving the *palki*, Guruji ordered some dry wood, upon which he put the beautiful *palki*. Guruji then set fire to the woods burning the entire *palki* and turning it into ashes. From the ashes the gold was separated and weighed, which was only 700 grams and the remaining 6,300 grams was copper. This means out of all the gold that he had collected from the Sikh congregations, *masand* Bulaki Das kept 90 per cent of it for his personal use. After this Guruji told *Mataji* that this was her most faithful and honest *masand* whose dishonesty with regards to the offering of Sikh *sangat* had been proved beyond doubt. 'These *masands* are indeed dishonest; they are not to be trusted any more.'[6]

A number of studies are available today on the problem of the *masands* and the challenges they posed to Sri Guru Gobind

Singhji. Madanjit Kaur has summed up the corruption of the *masands* in the following words:

> The *Masands* had deviated from their original assignment and Sikh ethics. They were indulging in evil practices and corruption and were misleading the Sikhs of their areas. Many *masands* had set themselves as Gurus in their districts and had begun to nominate their own successors. Instead of propagating Sikhism and forwarding the collation and offering for the devotees to the Guru's treasury, they were engaged in moneylending and trading on the offering, which they extorted from the local Sikhs.[7]

In sharp contrast stands the concept on which the *masands* were appointed originally from the time of Guru Amar Dasji as representatives of the Guru 'to exercise spiritual authority on behalf of the Guru, to receive offering from the Sikh and to preach Sikhism in designated areas'.[8]

The third major challenge, which all the ten Gurus faced was that of caste or *varna*. The Hindu society, particularly the Hill Rajas like Bhim Singh, was full of pride of being high caste. This can be seen in Raja Bhim Singh's statement made during the controversy about the *Parshadi Hathi* (an elephant given to Guruji as a token of his devotion by a king), which reads as 'The farmers (Jats) of lower caste, illiterate people, ironsmiths, traders, water carriers, haircutters, weavers, etc. are his Sikhs. We on the other hand are Rajputs of high caste. After becoming his followers we will not have any honour.'[9]

A biographer of Sri Guru Gobind Singhji, Sardar Surinder Singh Johar portrays a very clear picture of the caste system as practised at the time of Guruji. After describing the issue of the atrocities committed by Emperor Aurangzeb and the problem of *masands*, he writes about the caste situation of Guruji's time:

> Besides these factors, the Guru witnessed with his own eyes the fighting of the Hill Rajas among themselves without any cause whatsoever. They were not fighting for any principle. It was a fight among slaves for the retention of slavery and for the achievement of their personal ends. They sought assistance against their co-religionists from the Emperor. It was the height of degradation. Caste was dividing the entire race. The people thought only in terms of caste. The so-called low caste

people were hated and were not allowed even to enter any honourable professions. We know that once the Pandits of Banaras, even refused to teach Sanskrit to the Sikhs, as they thought it was below their dignity to teach them, for they belong to the low caste.[10]

Before we reflect on Guruji's vision of 'Universal Humanhood', let us recount the three major challenges faced by the tenth Guru. These were:

- To end/resist in full the tyrannical rule of Emperor Aurangzeb based upon the principle of religious fanaticism.
- To abolish the corrupted order of the *masands.*
- To eradicate or abolish caste practices among the Sikhs.

3. GURUJI'S VISION OF UNIVERSAL HUMANHOOD

After the martyrdom of the ninth Guruji as the rate of forced conversion of the Hindus and others into Islam increased, it became imperative for the tenth Guruji to do something concrete to stop Aurangzeb from committing extreme forms of atrocities. To meet such a huge challenge, an inclusive, astute and uncompromising ideology was needed, based on which an united force could be raised. With this in mind he introduced the idea of *Dharam Yuddh* (a battle of life, of ideals, righteousness, justice and truth),[11] that would draw even those who belong to other faiths including Hinduism and Islam. In the writings of the tenth Guruji in *Sri Dasam Granth Sahibji,* we encounter this clear vision of his with regard to *Dharam Yuddh* that is both resolute and universal in its approach.

We are actually concerned here with the vision and mission of an 'Apostle', the first question that may come to our mind is that who is an 'apostle', and why give this title to Sri Guru Gobind Singhji? The word 'apostle' originally comes from the Greek language which is derived from a verb *apostolo.* In secular usage it was used for 'a person sent on a specific assignment or mission'. In Greek it also some time means 'ambassador', 'delegate' or 'messenger'. Later it got a religious connotation and came into common usage in the Jew and Christian traditions. But the important point here for the purpose of this chapter's discussion is to note that one of the very essential qualifications of an 'apostle' was/is the 'divine call',[12] behind his mission. This qualification of an apostle applies to Sri Guru Gobind Singhji without any doubt, because according to his own testimony in *Bachitra Nataka*, the divine Ultimate Reality (*Akal Purakh*), has sent or given a call to Guruji to spread *dharma* (righteousness) in the world. In a *chaupai*, this is stated as follows:

Mai apnā suta tohi. Panthu parcura kala sāja.
Jāhi tahān tai dharmu calai. Kabudhi karana te loka haṭāi.

I have established you as my son and have created you to spread *dharma.*
Go from this place to that one,
move the cycle of *dharma* and stop people from committing evil deeds.[13]

After telling about his 'divine call', Guruji also stated the objective of his coming into this world. We have actually Guruji's mission statement in *Bachitra Nataka*. The English translation of his mission statement reads as follows:

Hama iha kaja jagata mo āe.
Dharama heta guradeva paṭhāe.
Jahan tahān dharama bithāro.
Dusata dokhayni pakari pacharo.
Yahī kāj dharā hama janaman.
Samjha lehu sādhū sabha manaman.
Dharama caḷāvana santa ubārana.
Dusata sabhana ko mūla upārina.

The Objective of my coming to this world is *dharma* and the Guru (Lord) has sent me for this purpose. Spread religion everywhere and throw down the knaves.
For this very purpose I have taken birth O Saints, this much you should understand well. I am born to spread religion, emancipate the saints and to wipe out the whole lot of wicked ones.[14]

What inspired Sri Guru Gobind Singhji to work relentlessly for his mission was in fact his vision of 'Universal Humanhood'. This vision of the unity of all human beings or humanity was as such common to all the ten Gurus. For example, in Japuji Sahib, Guru Nanak Devji has declared that before God all are equal:

Nānaka utamu nichu na koe

Saith Nanak: All before him are alike—
None high or low[15]

The third Guruji Amardasji made it clear that all human beings are created from the same source. He said:

Care varan akhāi sbhu koi.
Barhamu bind te sabh opati hoi.
Mati eka sagali sansāra.
Bahu bidhi bhānde ghṛāi kumāra.
Panc tatu mili dehi ka akāra.
Ghati vadhi ko karāi bicāra.

All talk of the four castes:
Know that all creation from the divine.
Essence has arisen.
The whole universal from the same day has appeared.[16]

As all the Gurus were extensions of the same Nanak, so was/ is their vision of 'Universal Humanhood'. In *Akal Usati* we find the tenth Guruji's vision of 'Universal Humanhood' in still more comprehensive and clearer terms:

Koū bhio mundīā, sannāsī koū jogī bhio.
Koū barhamacārī koū jatī anumānabo.
Hindū turaka koū rāphajī imāmasāphī.
Manas kī jati sobai ekai pahacānabo.
Karata karīm soī rājika rahīm oī.
Dūsro nā bheda koī bhūli bharma mānabo.
Eka hī kī seva sabha hī ko guradeva eka.
Eka hī sarūpa sabai ekai joti jānabo.

Some people (in the world) call themselves *mundia*, some *sannyasi* (ascetics), some *yogi* and some *yati* (celebrates). Some call themselves Hindu, some Turks (Muslim), some Hafzi and other Imamsafi. *But the* entire human kind should be recognised as one. The same one (Lord) is Creator, Compassionate Provider of bread, Munificient. He has no co-eternal, no dualism: we must never accept any duality. To serve the only one is our duty. He alone is the Guru of all. All mankind be taken as one manifestation of His Light.[17]

Guruji's vision of the 'Universal Humanhood' is rooted in his vision of *Akal Purakh* about whom he said in the opening verses of Japji:

Cakar cihan aru baran jātī aru pāti nahina jiha.
Rūpa ranga aru rekha bhekha koū kahi na sakata kiha.

You have no specific physical appearance, nor do you have any *varna*, caste or sub-caste. Nobody can describe your features, complexion, your outlines, or your garb.[18]

The length of this address will not allow us to go deeper into the 'vision and mission' of Sri Guru Gobind Singhji, therefore now we will steer our discussion to the next section which is on the formation of the 'institution of Khalsa'.

4. THE INSTITUTION OF KHALSA

In response to the threefold challenge enumerated in section two of this chapter Guru Gobind Singhji laid down the foundation of a 'new human order' based on his vision of 'Universal Humanhood'. This foundation was the 'institution of Khalsa'. How was this 'institution' or 'instrument' created? We have a number of sources, both primary and secondary which give concrete information about the formation of this institution. We shall recount here briefly the events leading to its formation as described in *Sri Dasam Guru Chamatkar*.[19]

On the Baisakhi day of CE 1699 (*Samvat* 1756), Guruji summoned a large gathering of Sikhs and when the *sangat* or congregation was in full swing, Guruji got up from his throne with his sword taken out from the sheath and addressed to the Sikh congregation, asking 'Is there any of my beloved Sikh, who is willing to give his head to me?' In the beginning nobody responded to Guruji's call. He repeated three times his call. Then one Sikh named Bhai Daya Ram, a Khatri of Lahore stood up and offered his head. Guruji took him inside a tent pitched for this purpose. Then Guruji repeated his call four more times, in response to which, a second Sikh, Bhai Dharm Das, a Jat from Delhi, came forward. The third Sikh who came forward was Bhai Mohkarm Chand, a washerman, the fourth Sikh was Bhai Chand of Bider, a barber, and the fifth Sikh was Bhai Himmat, a water-carrier by caste. That which at once flashes in our mind regarding these five Sikhs, whom Guruji later on called his five Beloved Ones (*Panj-Piyaras*), is that two of them were from the so-called high caste while the other three were from the so-called low caste. This event reminds us of the first Sikh theologian Bhai Gurdas, who said in his first *Var* about Guru Nanak Devji:

> (He made firm) the basis of the four pillars of *dharma*, and of the four varnas (castes) he created one.
> He regarded king and beggars as equal
> And caused the virtue of humility to be practised in the world.[20]

After declaring the five Beloved Ones as *Panj-Piyaras*, Guruji addressed them saying:

> I wish you all to embrace one creed and follow one path, obliterating all difference of religion. Let four Hindu castes, who have different rules for them in the *Shastras*, abandon them altogether and, adopting the way of co-operation, mix freely with one another. Let no one deem himself superior to another. Do not follow the old scriptures. Let none pay heed to the Ganga and other places of pilgrimages which are considered holy in the Hindu religion, or adore the Hindu deities, but all should believe in Guru Nanak and his successors. Let men of the four castes receive my baptism, eat out of the same vessel, and feel no disgust or contempt for one another.[21]

On the next day Guruji baptized the five Beloved Ones by administering them *amrit* (sugar water, stirred with a double-edged sword) out of the same bowl. In turn the Guru was baptized by them. After the baptism, Guruji declared the five Beloved Ones as the *Khalsa* meaning pure ones, and gave them new names with the suffix 'Singh' (meaning lion) for the males and 'Kaur' (meaning princess) for the female. Then the Guruji made them take oath to observe and wear the five K's: *kesh* (hair), *kangha* (comb), *kara* (a bracelet), *kachha* (a pair of shorts), and *kirpan* (a sword). They were also told not to smoke tobacco, consume alcoholic drinks, nor to eat meat slaughtered in the Muslim fashion (*halal*), but eat only *jhatka* meat (that is when the animal is killed outright with one blow) and not to have any extramarital relationship. After the baptism Guru greeted the five Beloved Ones with these words *'Wahe Guru ji ka Khalsa—Wahe Guru ji ki Fateh'* which means 'The *Khalsas* are the chosen people of God—Victory be to God.' Thus the Khalsa brotherhood was founded, which in future was to be an instrument and a model for 'Universal Humanhood'.

Let us now look at some of the views expressed by different scholars on Guruji's creating the institution of Khalsa. On one extreme is the view reflected by the authors of the *Encyclopedia of Sikh Religion and Culture* who say that,

> The *Khalsa* was founded by Gobind Rai, later Gobind Singh (tenth Guru). He preached the doctrine of the *Khalsa*. His teachings were calculated to convert the followers of Guru Nanak into a militant body without affecting their relationship with the Hindus, from whom the Sikh emerged, and to whom it was intended to protect. It is for this reason that the Hindus did not look upon Sikhism as a separate religion or social group.[22]

In contrast to this view, are the views of Sahib Kaur, which we find in her work *Sikh Thought*. She writes:

> From the very beginning the Gurus have worked against casteism among Sikhs. . . . Realizing that evil of casteism was again polluting the minds of Sikhs, Guru Gobind Singh's attack on casteism went much further. His baptism of the double-edged sword (*Khande-di-pahul*) was open to all, irrespective of caste. The holy water (*Amrit*) prepared for mass conversion was given to those who were taking initiative into the Khalsa Panth without any consideration of caste.[23]

There is a third view too, which Sardar Piara Singh 'Padam' has expressed in his work in Punjabi, the *Rahitnama*. His emphasis is on the problem of the *masands*. To quote from this work:

> Reason is very clear, because in the time of early Gurus, in every area *masands* were appointed to be the leaders of the Sikh congregations.

But soon their personal characters got corrupted, because they started using the *giving of Sikhs* (one-tenth) for their personal needs. In this way their order got distorted. After seeing such bad condition Guru Gobind Singhji took a revolutionary step and brought a complete change of Sikh congregation by bringing them directly in his hands and to this process Guruji named *Khalsa.*[24]

But perhaps the best holistic views about the Khasla we get from Prof. Puran Singh, which he has given in his work namely *The Book of the Ten Masters.* In it he says,

The creation of the Khalsa in India is the culmination of Guru Nanak's genius, and the written character of his Word. The Amritam of the Tenth Master completely transmuted the men drawn from a low or high castes of India, drawn from the Hindus or the Musalmans. After the Amritam, the Khalsa resembles no parent type of his own. For making the universal nation of man—for the evolution of one united family of men on earth, Gobind Singh had shown the way in his Khalsa.[25]

Another work which has brought the whole concept of the Khalsa closer to our present Indian society is that of Dr. Madanjit Kaur. She writes:

The basic idea behind the institution of the Khalsa, as conceived by Guru Gobind Singh, was to wipe out all invidious distinction between man and man and arouse the consciousness of human dignity even among those people who had all along been as fit only to occupy the fringes of society (the Dalits). Guru Gobind Singh's contribution was to give these ideas an institutional status. . . . The socio-political context of the amrit ceremony is also clearly a plebeian experiment. Three of the five beloved ones were Dalits. Even the Jats (Dharam was a Jat) in those days were considered only a cut above the dalits. . . . By asking the Sikhs to sip amrit from the same bowl, Guru Gobind was, in a way, inflicting the evil practice of Untouchability a fatal blow.[26]

With these views of Madanjit Kaur, who has rightly shown the relevance of the creation of Khalsa by the Apostle of 'Universal Humanhood' to our time, we move on to our next section.

5. CONTINUING CHALLENGE

At the close of discussion of this chapter, it may be good to re-affirm that the vision and mission of Sri Guru Gobind Singhji were most relevant to face the threefold challenge of his time. But this threefold challenge in some form continues even till today.

The first challenge which Guruji had was from the political forces like the fanaticism of Aurangzeb. To protect the religious freedom of the people of his time Guruji launched his mission. But this challenge is continuing up to this time, because there are millions of Indian citizens who even today are still not enjoying the fundamental and constitutional based religious freedom, given in Articles 15 and 25 of our Constitution.

The second challenge that the tenth Guruji faced was with regards to the corruption of the *masands*. To eliminate the corruption he brought the affairs of the Sikh *sangat* in his hands and after him he passed on the responsibility to the Khalsas. The problem of *masands* in all religions is in some form or the other prevalent even today.

The third challenge before Guruji was that of caste. All of us are well aware that in our society this cause is a continuing reality even today. Even all egalitarian faiths, including, Buddhism, Christianity and Islam, have got infected with the evils of the caste system. In some places in south India, there are different Christian churches and cemetries for different Christian communities. The same is true of the Sikh faith. Khushwant Singh in his book *The Sikhs Today,* while writing about the contemporary Sikh society says,

> Although all Sikhs have access to all Gurdwaras (where they sit together, and on festivals eat together), in the villages, the Sikh Harijans castes (*Mazhabis* or Dalit Sikhs) still suffer from discrimination. Amongst the 'upper' castes, there is little or no distinction except when it comes to arranging marriages.[27]

Similar views about the caste position among the Sikhs are expressed by W. Owen Cole and Piara Singh Sambhi in their book *The Sikh: Their Religious Beliefs and Practices*: 'Though

Sikhs will eat together in the *langar*, worship together and share *karah parshad*, marriages are still usually arranged between members of the same subgroup be it Arora, Ramgarhia or Jat.'[28]

6. CONCLUDING REMARKS

In conclusion, I want to emphasize that the message and challenge which we receive from Sri Guru Gobind Singhji through his vision and mission, which he has embodied in the Khalsa for the establishment of 'Universal Humanhood', is very much relevant even today and can make 'another world possible' for us—as against the forces of evils, that want to establish a 'unipolar world order' by controlling the economic, cultural and political powers using modern militarism—provided we are willing to work towards that end by considering one another as equal partners. The best example for this can be seen in Bhai Kanhaiya, who, when he was asked, why he was offering drinking water to the wounded soldiers of the enemy, replied to Guruji 'I always remembered your message and I am doing according to that only. In all the living beings which include "friends" or "enemies" I see my Guru's face everywhere.'[29]

NOTES

1. See for detailed discussion, C.H. Loehlin, *The Granth of Guru Gobind Singh and the Khalsa Brotherhood,* Lucknow, 1991, pp. 26-36.
2. Jodh Singh and Dharam Singh (trs.), *Sri Dasam Granth Sahib* (text and translation), Patiala, 2006, p. 151. (All the translated English verses of *Sri Dasam Granth Sahib* taken from this translation listed as *SDGS*.)
3. *SDGS*, p. 153.
4. Teja Singh Sodhi, *Sri Dasam Guru Chamtkaar* (Punjabi), Amritsar, 2006, p. 27.
5. Ibid., p. 86.
6. Ibid., pp. 38-9.
7. Madanjit Kaur, *Guru Gobind Singh: Historical and Ideological Perspective,* Chandigarh, 2007, p. 12.
8. Ibid., p. 150.
9. Teja Singh Sodhi, op. cit., p. 86.
10. Surinder Singh Johar, *Guru Gobind Singh: An Undying Spirit,* Delhi, 1999, p. 64.

11. Madanjit Kaur, op. cit., p. 128.
12. See for details of Greek meaning of 'apostle' on: William F, Arndt and F. Wilbur Gingrich, *A Greek-English Lexicon of the New Testament and Other Early Christian Literature*, Chicago, 1957, pp. 98-9. And *The New Bible Dictionary*, London, 1969, pp. 48-9.
13. *SDGS*, p. 159.
14. Ibid., p. 161.
15. *Sri Guru Granth Sahib*, p. 7.
16. Ibid., p. 1128.
17. *SDGS*, p. 55.
18. Ibid., p. 2.
19. See for detailed narration: Teja Singh Sodhi, op. cit., pp. 202-8.
20. Bhai Gurdasji, *Var I* in *Source on the Life and Teachings of Guru Nanak*, ed. Ganda Singh, Patiala, 1969, p. 33.
21. Surinder Singh Johar, op. cit., p. 66.
22. Ramesh Chandra Dogara and Gobind Singh Mansukhani, *Encyclopaedia of Sikh Religion and Culture*, Delhi, 1995, p. 258.
23. Sahib Kaur, *Sikh Thought*, Delhi, 1994, pp. 122-3.
24. Piara Singh Padam, *Rahinama* (Punjabi), Patiala, 1989, p. 22.
25. Puran Singh, *The Book of the Ten Masters*, Amritsar, 1995, p. 21.
26. Madanjit Kaur, op. cit., pp. 193-4.
27. Khushwant Singh, *The Sikhs Today*, Delhi, 1959, p. 24.
28. W. Owen Cole and Piara Singh Sambhi, *The Sikhs: Their Religion Beliefs and Practices*, Delhi, 1978, p. 138.
29. Teja Singh Sodhi, op. cit., p. 425.

PART TWO

IDENTITY

3

Early Sikh Faith: Counter-Religious Movements and Identity Formation

1. INTRODUCTORY REMARKS

The discussion of this chapter will be carried on under the following sub-heads: *one*, 'Counter-Religious Movement' and *two*, 'Formation of Sikh Identity'. The chapter will end with a brief concluding remarks on the continuing challenges to Sikh identity.

2. COUNTER-RELIGIOUS MOVEMENTS

This chapter is based upon the assumption that all religions before they took final shape or got organized, began as a movement. At that initial stage the founder of the religion would not even have declared his intention that he or she was going to begin a new faith. This was true of Buddhism and Lord Buddha, Jainism and Lord Mahavira, Judaism and Moses, Christianity and Lord Jesus Christ, Islam and Prophet Muhammad and also Sikhism and Guru Nanak Devji. All these faiths began when their founders started asking questions and offering alternative answers or giving meaning to the existing symbols, names, rituals, practices, etc.

Sometimes they even said 'no' to the existing traditions and offered an alternative. That was the time in each case when a 'movement' started taking shape, to later on become a 'counter-movement' (in the case of religion a 'counter-religious movement'). Here the expression 'counter' when added as a prefix to the word 'movement', as the *Concise Oxford Dictionary* puts, denotes 'movement or effect in the opposite direction'.[1]

If one reads the life of Guru Nanak Devji as stated in the Janam Sakhis, particularly his visit to the Hindu holy river Ganges in Hardwar[2] and his visit to Kaaba, the holy Muslim place in Mecca,[3] in both these incidents through his actions, he rejected the existing practices and views, and replaced them with new meaning (for details please refer chapter 6, section 1). He did not act just as an ordinary reformer or a revolutionary or an 'in between', as understood today by many scholars. In fact, the debate about Guru Nanak Devji being a reformer or a revolutionary and even about the early Sikh faith, whether it was a synthesis of two existing religious traditions, namely, 'Bhakti Hinduism' and 'Islamic Sufism' continues till today (*'Bhakti' denotes devotion and 'Sufism' mysticism in Islam*). A brief discussion on both these aspects is being offered to form our own view about the early Sikh faith.

First about the issue whether Guru Nanak Devji was a 'reformer' or a 'revolutionary'. There is one group, among which Gokul Chand Narain and Payne, were the main ones who behave that Guru Nanak Devji was only a reformer who did not reject the basic principles in Hinduism, but only wanted to remove the social and religious evil practices in Hinduism.[4] The second group, led by M.A. Macauliffe, Teja Singh and Bhai Kahan Singh, contend that Guru Nanak Devji was a revolutionary, because they believe Guru Nanak Devji wanted to replace the old Hindu societal structure with a new one.[5] There is also a third group, among whom the leading name is Kirpal Singh Narang, who hold the view that Guru Nanak Devji was neither a reformer nor a revolutionary, but somewhere 'in between'. According to them, Guru Nanak Devji's new religion though different from some of the basic tenets of the Hindu religion, was not totally against it.[6]

Here, in these above views reference has been made only to Hindu religion, but as referred to earlier, Guru Nanak Devji was equally concerned about Islam, because these were the two major religions which were during his time. It is also true that the Sikh faith in the beginning was part of a worldwide re-awakening and revival movement of the middle ages (fifteenth and sixteenth century). In India during this period (because majority of the people showed dissatisfaction with the old and rigid and ritualistic ways of the existing religions), a movement known as the Bhakti movement both among the followers of Hinduism and Islam, became flourished. The Hindu leaders of the Bhakti movement, included Sri Chaitanya and Mira Bai, while Muslim mystic leaders included Sheikh Farid and Kabir. Guru Nanak Devji's teachings had several commonalities with the Hindu Bhakti saints as well as with the Muslim Sufi saints. For instance, they all used the language of the masses, rejected caste distinctions and also rituals and ceremonies. All of them lay stress on morality and purity of the heart. It could be that because of these commonalities between both the groups, that Edhne K. Marenco concluded about Guru Nanak Devji that 'The culmination of the Sufi movement of the Muslims and Bhakti movement of the Hindus was to be found in the doctrines of Guru Nanak.'[7]

However, there are some scholars who entirely reject the idea of Sikh faith as a synthesis of Hindu Bhakti and Muslim Sufism. Among them is a well-known scholar W.H. Mcleod. According to him, these two religious traditions only had a marginal effect on Guru Nanak Devji's teachings. Instead, the major influence upon him was of Sant (Saint) tradition which followed Vaishnava Bhakti, who rejected all forms of idol worship, rituals, temples, pilgrimage and caste. They also used the local language.[8] But Mcleod's understanding of Nath tradition or Sant tradition is also questionable because Nath Yogis demand complete physical discipline and it is true they outwardly admit God and call him Krishna and Chaitanya just as Vaishnavas do, but in truth they have no concern with God. Each Yogi is God in the universe of his body.[9] No such thoughts, however, have a place in Guru Nanak Devji's teachings. In fact, Guru Nanak Devji had even basic difference with the Bhakti saints and sufis, who stressed more on renunciation, whereas Guru Nanak Devji stressed on family life. Towards the end of his life Guru Nanak Devji appointed a successor to keep the continuity of his faith, whereas no such tradition is there among Bhakti or Sufi saints. All these clearly indicate that Sikh faith from the very beginning was in the real sense a counter-religious movement, which today has taken the form of a full-fledged religion, though much younger in age as compared to other world religions.

3. FORMATION OF A SIKH IDENTITY

The Sikh movement was founded by Guru Nanak Devji, who was born on 15 April 1469, in village Nankana Sahib, about 65 km from Lahore (now in Pakistan). As a young boy he studied under both a Hindu and a Muslim teacher. He was always interested in spending time in the company of religious saints belonging to different religious faiths. But no one could satisfy his inner quest. So one day he left home. He prayed and meditated intensely and kept thinking of the bitter differences between Hindus and Muslims. It's at that stage of his life that he was led to a very radical belief: 'There is no Hindu, there is no Musalman.'[10] After this enriching experience he took two companions, one, a Muslim named Mardana and the other a Jat Hindu called Bala. He called them *bhai*, meaning brothers. Mardana was a musician. Guru Nanak Devji used to compose his messages which Mardana set to music and then they would sing them. Guru Nanak Devji used the local dialect or language. His simple teaching appealed to the Punjabi villagers and within a short time Guru Nanak Devji had several disciples.

There were nine other Gurus after Guru Nanak Devji. Guru Nanak Devji appointed one of his disciples named Lehana as his successor. Lehana's name was changed to Angad, which means 'limb' in English, indicating thereby that he was an extension of the former Guru. Each Guru further strengthened the Sikh movement started by Guru Nanak Devji and also made specific contributions to the growth of the Sikh religion, which later on helped in establishing a distinct Sikh identity. Guru Angad (CE 1539-52) the second, Guru popularized the Gurmukhi script, which greatly helped in the development of the Punjabi language. This was the script which was used later on for the writing Sikh scriptures. It is different from the Devanagari script, which is used to write Sanskrit, which was the language of the priestly class of the Hindus, and today Hindi is written in Devanagari script.

Guru Angadji appointed as his successor Guru Amar Dasji, who was one of his disciples. Guru Amar Dasji served as Guru for years (CE 1552-74). By the time of Guru Amar Dasji, the Sikh movement had spread all over rural Punjab, particularly among the farmers of Punjab accepted the Guru's faith. In the future to come, these Jat villagers contributed much to the growth of Sikh faith. As the Sikh faith was spreading, a proper organization was needed. In order to fulfil this need, Guru Amar Dasji set-up 22 centres and appointed lay preachers to take care of each centre. He also commissioned 146 well-trained missionaries, of which 94 were men and 52 were women,[11] the latter was indeed a bold step on his part. Guru Amar Dasji also made popular the institution of the *langar* or free kitchen in Gurdwaras (Sikh temples), where people of all caste and class can share common meals. He also founded for the Sikhs a centre of pilgrimage at Goindwal on the banks of river Beas. He introduced forms of Sikh marriage ceremonies and festivals which were different from those of Hindus. These steps were to add toward the beginning of a separate Sikh identity.

The fourth Guru, Guru Ram Dasji who succeeded Guru Amar Dasji made a significant contribution. He laid the foundation of the Sikh holy city of Ramdaspur, which later came to be known as Amritsar. Arjan Devji (CE 1581-1606) the fifth Guru was born in 1563 at Goindwal. The youngest son of Guru Ram Dasji, he was a great builder. The famous Golden Temple in Amritsar today, which is the main pilgrimage centre for the Sikhs has been built by him. The foundation for this great temple was laid by a Muslim saint. Besides being a good builder, Guru Arjan Devji was also poet and scholar. His greatest work was the compilation of the

Adi Granth (Sikh Scripture) in 1604. It includes the writings of the first four Gurus along with his own. He also included therein the writings of both Hindu and Muslim saints. The compilation of the *Adi Granth* was a major step for the future of the Sikh religion. This holy scripture of the Sikhs is the base for all religious and other matters. By Guru Arjan Devji's time the Sikh community had grown in number and had become much more robust. Jahangir did not like this. He arrested Guruji and tortured to death in Lahore in 1606. Thus Guru Arjan Devji became the first important martyr in Sikh history.

After Guru Arjan Devji's death, his son Hargobind became the Guru in 1606 and lived till 1645. During his time, a turning point in Sikh history came. Guru Arjan Devji's execution and growing hostility towards the Sikh movement forced Guru Hargobindji to prepare his followers to defend themselves by military means. In fact, Guru Arjan Devji already had prepared him for this and had asked Bhai Budda to train Guru Hargobindji as a soldier-saint. So after becoming Guru, to give lead to his followers, he himself wore two swords, a symbol of the spiritual (*Piri*) and the temporal (*Miri*) powers. He also combined the symbols of service, the *Deg* (the cauldron to serve to the needy), and *Tegh* (the sword to defend the helpless). He asked his followers to adopt this as their life principle. This, according to Ganda Singh, was the first step towards the transformation of the Sikh religion and, by extension the community into a militant church.[12]

The seventh Guru, Har Raiji, was Guru from 1645 till 1661. He further developed a fighting force of 2,200 horsemen, and also organized the missionary preaching work outside the Punjab. The eighth Guru, Har Kishanji, was only five years old, when he became the Guru. He went to Delhi in response to the summons of Emperor Aurangzeb where he contracted small-pox and died in 1664. His last words were: 'Baba Bakale' which means that his successor should to be found at a place in the Punjab.

The ninth Guru, Tegh Bahadurji, was the youngest son of Guru Hargobindji; he became Guru in 1664. A zealous preacher, Guru Tegh Bahadur was also a great champion of religious freedom.

To get freedom of worship for the Hindu Brahmins, he incurred the wrath of the Muslim Emperor Aurangzeb, who asked the Guru to either accept Islam or face death. But the Guru refused, and he was beheaded on 11 November 1675, in Delhi.

After his father's martyrdom, Gobind Singhji became Guru in 1675. He was only ten years old when he became Guru. He spent years studying Persian, Sanskrit, Punjabi, Hindi and learning the art of war.

At long last came the greatest day in Sikh history. In March CE 1699, at the time of Baisakhi festival, the Guruji assembled his followers at Anandpur Sahib and selected in a dramatic manner five beloved ones known as *Panj-Piyaras*. The Guruji baptized these five by administering them *amrit* and out of the same bowl, the Guru in turn was baptized by them. After the baptism, the Guruji declared the five beloved ones as *Khalsa*, meaning pure ones, and gave them new names with a common suffix ('Singh' meaning 'lion' for men and 'Kaur' meaning 'princess' for women). The Guruji also made them take an oath to observe and wear what came to be called the five K's: *kesh* (hair), *kangha* (comb), *kara* (bracelet), *kachha* (a pair of shorts), and *kirpan* (a sword). After his baptism the Guru greeted the five beloved ones with these words *Wahe Guruji Ka Khalsa—Wahe Guruji Ki Fateh* which means 'Khalsa are the chosen people of God, victory be to God.' Thus the Khalsa brotherhood was founded and the final stage of militarization of Sikhism was completed. (See for detail discussion in chapter 2, section 4 on 'The Institution of Khalsa.) But we must remember that the Guruji himself never waged a battle first. He always fought to protect his followers. While writing to Emperor Aurangzeb, he wrote in his Epistle of Victory known as the *Zafarnama* 'Helplessly, as a last resort, I came forward and took arms. When all other means have failed, it is lawful to resort to the sword' (21: 22).

Thus Guru Gobind Singhji gave the final form to the Sikh religion. He had already transferred the physical leadership of the Sikh movement to the representatives of the community, elected or selected on the basis of their devotion to the Guruji's teachings. Along with this, before his death, he also announced that he would have no human successor. Instead of that, the *Guru Granth Sahib* (the *Adi Granth*) will be the only Guru of the Sikhs. To the *Adi Granth* he added 116 hymns written by his father Guru Tegh Bahadurji, and one of his own, known as *Sri Guru Granth Sahibji*. In this way the process which had begun about two hundred years back was now completed.

It is true that the three factors: a regular and recognized succession, the permanent form of the teachings of Gurus and other saints (*Shri Guru Granth Sahibji*) and the founding of the Khalsa were major steps toward building a separate and distinct Sikh identity. But at the same time, a number of followers of Guru Nanak Devji known as Nanak-panthis did not accept the baptism of Guru Gobind Singhji and therefore did not become *keshdhari* (having hair), instead, they continued to be *sahajdhari* Sikhs (without hair). Also there were no rigid dividing lines between the *keshdhari* and *sahajdhari* Sikhs. About this Rajiv Kapur says:

> In the everyday socio-religious life of the Sikhs, however, the acceptance of Khalsa baptism did not set the *Keshdhari* Sikhs apart from the Hindu community. Even when the Khalsa Sikhs established a powerful Kingdom in the Punjab, their rulers continued to observe Hindu rituals and traditions in addition to Sikh practices.[13]

4. CONCLUDING REMARKS

It is true that Sikh faith began as a 'counter-religious movement' with an open declaration about the existing two major religious traditions that 'There is no Hindu, there is no Musalman'. Besides, what all the Gurus contributed in the formation of Sikh identity, three major factors: namely, a regular and recognized succession, the permanent canonized scripture (*Shri Guru Granth Sahibji*) and the founding of the Khalsa, contributed by Guru Nanak Devji, Guru Arjan Devji and Guru Gobind Singhji respectively, gave the final shape to an independent identity of Sikhism as a religion. Therefore Sikh faith as it stands today is a religion in its own right with a very distinctive identity.

But a fact here that needs to be noted is that as in the case of all other living faiths, Sikh faith continues to face challenges both within and from outside it. For instance, caste is one such issue against which all the Gurus spoke both in words and action. The very fact that among the first five members of Khalsa, four belonged to the lowest castes (as seen in chapter 2) and the tenth Guru Gobind Singhji addressed an untouchable Bhai Jiwan Singh as 'Guru ka Beta' (son of a Guru). The purpose behind giving a single common surname 'Singh' (lion) to all male Sikhs and 'Kaur' (princess) to all women Sikhs was to get rid of caste distinction forever. But sadly, separate caste-based Sikh Gurdwaras (temples), particularly in villages in Punjab and marriage within the caste-based communities continues to pose challenges to the Sikh identity or Sikh community as a whole. Towards the end of the nineteenth century, reformation started to deal with such issues gave birth to the Singh Sabha in 1873, but the problems mentioned above still continues.

The other serious challenge is more political in nature, particularly in the present time. To stay in power, many political Sikh leaders continue to compromise even with their faith identity. In one way this was also a continuing problem, as Rajiv Kapur has pointed out about some of the Khalsa Sikh rulers in the past. Even today some time similar mistakes are being made while interpreting Article 25 of the Indian Constitution, where Sikh Gurdwaras are equated with the Hindu temples.

Finally there are new challenges coming, brought out by the processes of modernization and globalization, through which new classes in the every human society are getting introduced and the dividing line between the rich and the poor are increasing. New value systems are being introduced. To this new situation every living faith community has to respond. It is yet to be seen how the Sikh community will respond to this new situation. In the next chapter, a specific case of the Punjab issue is discussed, which is a good example of the continuing struggle for a Sikh identity.

NOTES

1. Catherine'Soanes, and Angus Stevenson (eds.), *Concise Oxford English Dictionary*, 11th edn. (rev.), Oxford, 2007, p. 326.
2. W.H. Mcleod (ed.), *The 40 Janam Sakhi,* Amristar, 1980, pp. 83-5.
3. Bhai Vir Singhji (ed.), *Puratan Janam Sakhi* (in Punjabi), Amritsar, 1971, pp. 182-7.
4. S. Kirpal Singh Narang, 'Guru Nanak: Sudharak Jan Krantikari' (in Punjabi) in *Punjabi Dunia,* Guru Nanak Ank (Part One), Patiala, n.d., pp. 61-2.
5. Ibid., pp. 63-5.
6. K.C. Gupta, *Guru Nanak: Krantikari* (in Punjabi), pp. 162-3.
7. Edhne Marenco, *The Trnsformation of Sikh Society*, Delhi, 1976, p. 24.
8. W.H. Mcleod, *The Evolution of the Sikh Community,* Delhi, 1975, pp. 6-7.
9. Haridas Bhattacharyya (ed.), *The Cultural Heritage of India,* vol. IV (*The Religions*), Calcutta, 1983, p. 280.
10. Bhai Vir Singh (ed.), *Puratan Janam Sakhi*, op. cit., p. 43.
11. Trilochan Singh, *Guru Nanak: Founder of Sikhism,* Delhi, 1969, p. 11.
12. Ganda Singh, 'The Sikh: A Historical Intepretation', in *Religion and Society*, CISRS, vol. XI, no.1, March 1964, p. 24.
13. Rajiv A. Kapur, *Sikh Separation: The Politics of Faith*, London, 1986, pp. 5-6.

4

Struggle for Identity Continues (1985-1995)

1. INTRODUCTORY REMARKS

Challenges to Religious Pluralism—Sikhism is perhaps one of the most well-known subjects—which in different forms is a major concern during the post-Independence era in Indian history. For some, it has become a threat to the very fabric of the existence of our Indian pluralistic society. But for others it is a struggle for maintaining or establishing one's own religious identity while still living in a pluralistic society. After all, pluralism is basically a concept, which upholds the principle of tolerance of diversities, including differences of opinion, views, beliefs and attitudes. The Punjab issue or the Sikh problem of 1985-95 has to be seen in the light of this understanding of 'religious pluralism' because, in our country some are working towards building a totalitarian society by introducing not only a dominant language, but also 'a majority religion and a monolithic set of norms'.[1] In this chapter the Punjab issue is examined from the angle of the latter view, which actually should be considered a continuing discussion, in which we saw the historical background of the development of Sikh identity.

The Punjab issue was one of the most important issues which our country was faced during 1985-95. At that time one could find some information almost everyday about it in all kinds of media at the national level. Based upon what the media told us, some of us had offered very simplistic formulae of explanation of this on-going issue. One of the results of these simplistic formulae was that most of the owners of such formulae either start condemning a particular community or started showing contempt toward the members of that community. Such approaches to an issue like the Punjab one only helps to aggravate the intensity of the problem, which ultimately also became a threat to the harmony of a pluralistic society like ours.

The Punjab issue, was actually a question of Sikh identity and how to sustain the same. Behind this issue, there were a number of religious, social, political and economic factors. All these factors have a long history behind them, beginning with the birth of its founder Guru Nanak Devji in 1469. Therefore to deal with this centuries-old question, one brief essay is not sufficient. It needs volumes of works (some have already been written and a few are referred to in this chapter). Anyhow, in order to formulate our own opinion, a brief discussion on the historical development of the Punjab problem is made hereunder the following heads:

- Early period;
- British period;
- Post-Independence period; and
- Comments.

2. EARLY PERIOD

The 'early period' begins with the birth of Guru Nanak Devji in CE 1469 and ends with the martyrdom of Guru Gobind Singhji in 1708. The ten Gurus' lives run almost parallel to the Mughal (Muslim) rule. The contribution made by each Guru to the development to Sikh faith is discussed in detail in chapter 3, under the subheads 'Formation of Sikh Identiy'. This essay is actually an extension of chapter 3. As a detailed discussion on the 'early period' has already taken place in chapter 3, therefore, here we will begin the discussion with the 'British period, which followed the 'Muslim period' as well as on the Ten Guru's like time period in which the formation of 'Sikh Identity' took a full form, but threat to Sikh identiy continues even in our time, reference to which was also made in the concluding section of chapter 3.

3. THE BRITISH PERIOD

According to Pranay Gupte, 'The genesis of the Sikh-Hindu polarization of the 1980s dates back to the last century, when the British successfully sowed the seeds of mutual suspicion among the members of the two communities.'[2] Pranay Gupte's view may be partly correct, because as can be seen in the discussion in the section on 'Formation of Sikh Identity' in chapter 3, the historical roots of the struggle for a separate Sikh identity goes back much earlier than the British period. So, we agree with Pranay Gupte's views only partly because it is certainly true that the issue of a separate Sikh identity became more focused and sharpened during the British period for which many factors are responsible. Here we will refer only to three such factors, which include the policy of census, the policy of recruitment in the army, and the Gurdwara Reform Movement.

3.1 *Policy of Census*

As we all know it was the British who introduced the census system, which, according to some historians, gave birth to the 'politics of numbers' and also helped a number of communities in India to establish their identities.[3] The same effect of the census struck the Sikh community too. For example, the first census of the Punjab took place in 1855. At that time, except for the districts of Amritsar, Gurdaspur, Sialkot, Lahore and Gujranwala (where Sikhs were enumerated separately), at all other places, the Sikhs and the Hindus were counted together. By the time of the next census in 1868, the number of Sikhs increased substantially (from 181,172 in 1855 to 511,064 in 1868). In 1881, the Sikhs were numbered separately from the Hindus in the Punjab. But because of the Hindu influence, the Sikh Dalit converts were treated as Hindus and in those days they were also not permitted to enter the Gurdwaras. The census also revealed how much the Christian missionaries' work was effective, especially in increasing the number of Christians from Dalit background. The number of Christians in 1881 was 3,796; in 1891 it was 19,547; in 1901 it was 37,980; in 1911 it was 163,994, and in 1921 it was 315,931. By that time the educated section of the Sikhs were deeply distressed with the ongoing Sikh social and religious practices. Some even became Christians. The Sikhs faced a similar threat from the Arya Samaj, which was founded at Rajkot in Gujarat in 1875; in 1883 it was established in the Punjab. The Arya Samaj not only started a reform among the Hindus, but also the practice of *shuddhikaran* (a ritual of purification). Through this practice, they not only attempted to bring back Christian Dalits to the Hindu fold, but also re-converted Sikh Dalits to Hinduism in August 1896.[4]

About this new situation created by the census policy Kapur has rightly pointed out:

> The reform of behavioural Sikhism to renew its vitality, the need to safeguard it from Christian inroads and the preservation of a distinct Sikh identity were for many of these Sikhs no longer a means of intellectual concern, they had become a practical necessity.[5]

3.2 *The Recruitment Policy*

After the death of the Sikh Maharaja Ranjit Singh, Punjab was annexed by the British in 1849. But in the Second Anglo-Sikh War (1848-9), the Britishers also came to appreciate the bravery of their opponents. The Sikhs therefore were encouraged by the British rulers. As a result the Sikhs (at the time of 1857 Mutiny) fought along with the Britishers against the other Indians. A legend attributed to the tenth Guru Gobind Singhji was widely circulated. According to this legend: 'the English shall possess great power and the combined armies of the English and the Sikhs shall be very powerful as long as they rule with united councils'.

According to Kapur, because of the nature of British-Sikh relationship, 'The army had from the outset defined Sikh to mean *keshdhari* Sikhs, and had actively encouraged the maintenance of the *keshdharis* separate identity' (Kapur 1986, p. 24). Because of such actions of the Britishers, some followers of the Gurus began to consider themselves as distinct from the Hindus, i.e. 'as Sikhs, Keshdhari and Sahajdhari; others believed that Sikhism was a sect of Hinduism and considered themselves to be Sikh-Hindu'.[6]

3.3 *Gurdwara Reform Movement*

During the British period, a number of Hindu practices, including the worship of gods and goddesses, were going on among the Sikhs. Even the practice of caste system was openly followed by the Sikhs. Christian missionaries and later the members of Arya Samaj took advantage of this situation. As pointed out earlier, because of these problems, even the educated Sikhs got attracted towards Christianity. To meet the challenge of this situation, some Sikhs started working towards reform of the Sikh community. These included the Nirankari, Namdhari or the Kuka sect. Later, in 1873, these movements gave birth to a society known as the Singh Sabha. Along with other objectives, this society's main objective was to arouse a love of religion among the Sikhs and 'to propagate the true Sikh religion everywhere'. In the beginning these Sabhas were started as independent organs in different cities such as Amritsar (1873), Lahore (1879) and by 1899 there were 121 Singh Sabhas functioning all over the Punjab. The members of these Sabhas even started *Shuddhi sabhas* like the Arya Samajis in order to bring back converts from other religions to the Sikh fold. Such efforts had their repercussions:

> Bitter debate between Aryas and the Hindus over the demarcation of communal boundaries only added fuel to the passion with which the Sikh reformers advocated the distinctiveness of a Sikh identity. Indeed, within a few years Sikh reformers who espoused the cause of a separate Sikh identity, the Tat, or true Khalsa as they came to be called, had become the dominant group among active Singh Sabhaites.[7]

In the meanwhile, the number of Singh Sabhas increased and with them their related activities. To coordinate all these activities, an organization known as Chief Khalsa Diwan was formed in 1902.

One of the main steps undertaken by the Singh Sabha was in the area of social and religious reform, which was connected with the management of the Sikh gurdwaras. During the rule of the Muslim emperors in Delhi, the Sikh community had to face bitter persecution and its members were forced to go into exile. During that period the management of the gurdwara was passed on to the hands of the Udasi sect founded by Guru Nanak's eldest son Sri Chand. A large number of members of this sect were *sahajdhari* Sikhs, who knew the Sikh scripture well, but in many ways they were practising Hindus also. However, they continued to serve as *granthis* and *mahants* in Sikh gurdwaras. Because of the large income from gurdwaras, these *mahants* became corrupt and necessitated reform in the management of gurdwaras.

At the same time, the Sikhs had also become aware of their political identity and separate rights. They demanded special representation, which in principle was accepted by the Montague-Chelmsford Commission in 1918. In order to deal with the political issues related to the Sikhs, they founded the Central Sikh League on 30 December 1919. Through the establishment of the Central Sikh League, Tat Khalsa started working towards Khalsa nationalism.

In 1920, the militant members of course re-named the Gurdwara Committee as the Shiromani Gurdwara Prabandhak Committee (SGPC), which later on instituted an organization known as the Shiromani Akali Dal. This new body was supposed to implement all the works of SGPC. However, the management of gurdwaras continued to be in the hands of the *mahants* and *pujaris*. But organized Akalis now became a big threat to the authority of these *mahants*. On the other hand, the *mahants* refused to recognize the authority of SGPC; instead, they started another organization known as the Udasi Mahamandal, in order to protect their rights. But in various ways the Akalis continued to work for taking over the gurdwara management. Some of the gurdwaras were taken over by force.

The biggest threat was faced by the management of Nankana Sahib Gurdwara in the Lahore district, which was the birth place of Guru Nanak. Its *mahant*, Narain Das, first approached the British government for protection, but later he took the entire matter into his own hands. He hired *gundas* and when in February 1921, an Akali Jatha went to take over the gurdwara, Narain Das's men opened fire on the Jatha and killed 130 men. These men were hacked to pieces and some were even burnt alive. This incident provoked the government to intervene in the management of the gurdwara. Narain Das and seven men were arrested and were sentenced to life.

Finally a draft bill, the Sikh Gurdwara and Shrine Bill was prepared in 1922. According to Rajiv Kapur:

> On the surface the bill seemed an equitable solution to the controversy over Gurdwara management. But the Punjab government had made a crucial concession in the bill to mean a person who professes the Sikh faith, and the bill laid down that a person would or would not be deemed to be a Sikh depending on whether or not he makes a declaration stating: I solemnly affirm that I am a Sikh, that I believe in the Guru Granth Sahib, that I believe in the Ten Gurus and that I have no other religion.[8]

With this declaration no more *sahajdhari* Sikh could claim they were Hindu as well as Sikh, because the above bill becomes an Act in 1922.

After this, on 8 July 1925, the Sikh Gurdwara Act was passed, which

> marked a turning point in the movement towards the reformulation of Sikh identity and the development of a distinct Sikh Communal consciousness. The Sikh Gurdwara Act of 1925 has since undergone thirty amendments, but its basic principles and the institutions established under it have remained the same.

In the meanwhile, till Independence, a number of other events led the country to freedom. But at the time of the creation of Pakistan, through the mediation of Tara Singh the idea of separate Sikh State of Sikhistan or Khalistan was officially accepted by the Akali Dal in March 1946.[9]

4. POST-INDEPENDENCE

This period from 1947 till date is known to all, particularly the Indians. During this period also the identity struggles among different religious communities are continuing. Here for our discussion only a brief reference to some of the incidents and documents is made.

The first document which created a post-Independence controversy with regard to the identity among various religious communities was the Constitution (Scheduled Castes) Order 1950 (also known as the 1950 Presidential Order), which, in the beginning only recognized the identity of Dalit Hindus (Scheduled Castes). One interpretation, particularly from the Bharatiya Janata Party, is that 'under the Constitution Buddhists and Sikhs and Jains were classified as Hindus'.[10] But this was not accepted by the Sikh community and they struggled on behalf of the Dalit Sikhs demanding that they should be recognized as a separate group as 'Sikhs'; this demand of theirs was accepted in 1956 and the Presidential Order was suitably amended by the Parliament.[11]

Concerning the separate or autonomous Sikh state, according to some well-known scholars, the idea of a separate nation 'started taking shape with Nehru's announcement that new Indian states would be created along linguistic lines'. Accordingly, 13 linguistically based states were created, but the Punjab was ignored. Therefore, in April 1960, the Akali Dal launched a movement for Punjabi Sabha. This demand was accepted in 1966, and a separate state of Punjab was created by dividing the earlier Punjab into three states: Haryana, in which 5 per cent Sikhs lived, Himachal Pradesh where 2 per cent Sikhs lived, and the present Punjab where about 52 per cent Sikhs lived.[12]

The struggle for greater autonomy of course continued along with some other demands which included both religious and political. For example, the famous 'Political Goal Resolution' of Anandpur Sahib, which was adopted by the Working Committee of the Akali Dal on 16-17 October 1973, spelt out a number of demands such as some of the Punjabi-speaking areas left out from the Punjab should be given back, the Indian Constitution should be recast on real federal principles, the centre's powers should be restricted to defence, foreign relations, currency and general communication, etc. The ideology and the objectives of the Akali Dal were stated in the preamble of the Resolution thus:

> The political goal of the panth, without doubt, is enshrined in the commandments of the 10th Lord, in the pages of Sikh history and in the very heart of the Khalsa panth, the ultimate objective of which is the pre-eminences of the Khalsa.[13]

The *Ludhiana Resolution*, which was adopted by All India Akali Conference in its meeting held on 28 and 29 October 1978, adopted a resolution in 'the light of the Anandpur Sahib Resolution', which included the following six demands:

(a) Chandigarh, originally raised as a capital for Punjab, should be handed over to Punjab.
(b) The long-standing demand of the Shiromani Akali Dal for merger with Punjab of the Punjabi-speaking areas to be identified by linguistic experts with the village as a unit should be conceded.
(c) The control of headworks should continue to be vested in the Punjab and, if need be, the Reorganisation Act should be amended.
(d) The arbitrary and unjust award given by Mrs. Indira Gandhi during the emergency, on the distribution of Ravi-Beas waters should be revised on the universally accepted forms and principles and justice should be done to the Punjab.
(e) Keeping in view the special aptitude and martial qualities of the Sikhs, the present ratio of their strength in the army should be maintained.
(f) The excesses being committed on the settlers in the Terai region of U.P. in the name of land reforms should be stopped by making suitable amendments to the ceiling law on the basis of central guidelines.[14]

It was followed by the *White Paper on the Punjab Agitation,* New Delhi on 10 July 1984, which has identified the following four factors responsible for the Punjab situation:

- The agitations sponsored by the Shiromani Akali Dal in support of certain demands which had been submitted to the government and on which negotiations were in progress;

- A stridently communal and extremist movement which degenerated into open advocacy of violence and sanction for the most heinous crimes against innocent and helpless citizens and against the state;
- Secessionist and anti-national activities with the declared objective of establishing an independent state for the Sikhs with external support; and
- Involvement of criminals, smugglers, other anti-social elements and Naxalites who took advantage of the situation for their own ends.[15]

Then came the 11-Point Agreement between Prime Minister Rajiv Gandhi, and the Akali Dal Chief Harcharan Singh Longowal, which was signed on 24 July 1985, regarding the Punjab problem. Part of this Agreement is reproduced here, which deals with the main issues related to the Punjabi problem.

4.1 *Territorial Claims*

The capital project area of Chandigarh will go to the Punjab. Some adjoining areas which were previously part of the Hindi or the Punjabi-speaking regions were included in the Union Territory. With the capital region going to Punjab the areas which were added to the Union Territory from the Punjabi regions of the erstwhile state of Punjab will be transferred to Punjab and those from Hindi region to Haryana. The entire Sukhna lake will be kept as part of the Chandigarh area and will thus go to Punjab.

It had always been maintained by Mrs Indira Gandhi that when Chandigarh will to go to the Punjab some Hindi-speaking territories in Punjab will go to Haryana. A commission will be constituted to determine the specific Hindi-speaking areas of Punjab which should go to Haryana, in lieu of Chandigarh.

The principle of contiguity and linguistic affinity with a village as a unit will be the basis of such determination. The commission will be required to give its findings by 31 December 1985 and these will be binding on both sides. The work of the commission will be limited to this aspect and will be distinct from the general boundary claims.

The actual transfer of Chandigarh to the Punjab and areas in lieu thereof to Haryana was proposed to take place simultaneously on 26 January 1986.

There were other claims and counter-claims for readjustment of the existing Punjab-Haryana boundaries. The government will appoint another commission to consider these matters and give its findings. Such findings will be binding on the concerned states. These terms of reference will be based on a village as a unit, linguistic affinity and contiguity.

4.2 *Centre-State Relations*

Shiromani Akali Dal stated that the Anandpur Sahib Resolution is entirely within the framework of the Indian Constitution; that it attempts to define the concept of centre-state relations in a manner which may bring out the true federal characteristics of our Unitary Constitution; and that the purpose of the Resolution is to provide greater autonomy to the state with a view to strengthening the unity and integrity of the country, since unity in diversity forms the cornerstone of our national entity.

In view of the above, the Anandpur Sahib Resolution insofar as it dealt with centre-state relations, stands referred to the Sarkaria Commission.

4.3 *Sharing of River Waters*

The farmers of Punjab, Haryana and Rajasthan will continue to get water not less than what they are using from the Ravi-Beas system as on 1 July 1985. Waters used for consumptive purposes will also remain unaffected. The quantum of usage claimed shall be verified by the Tribunal referred to below. The claim of Punjab and Haryana regarding their share in the remaining waters will be referred for adjudication to a Tribunal to be presided over by a Supreme Court judge. The decision of this Tribunal will be rendered within six months and would be binding on both parties. All legal and constitutional steps required in this respect should be taken expeditiously.

The construction of the SYL canal shall continue. The canal shall be completed by 15 August 1986.[16]

In conclusion, here is an excerpt from the report published by the *Indian Express* on the formation of the new united Akali Party on 2 May 1994. It said:

> The formation of the new party came into being after seven days of continuous deliberations held by frontline leaders of these factions and SGPC President G.S. Tohra at Akal Takht, in the presence of five Sikh high priests headed by the acting head priest of Akal Takht, Manjit Singh pledging to wage a struggle for a 'separate area' (within India) where Sikhs can experience the glow of freedom.

The same newspaper dated 3 May 1994, in its editorial, entitled 'Back to Mischief' gave its judgement on the above Akali unity move as follows:

> There are no two ways about the fact that the so-called Amritsar Declaration is mischievous in the extreme and inimical to the interests of the people of Punjab. Once again there is the pretence of seeking autonomy for Punjab accompanied by rhetoric about the right to a Sikh homeland and undercurrents of religious grievance. Once again the Akalis are playing with fire. . . . But if the alternative is the new Shiromani Akali Dal with a one-point trouble-making programme, Punjab is better off without it. . . . *Miri* and *Piri*, the traditional Akali route to power, has been the ruin of the Akalis. . . .

5. COMMENTS

The historical background to the Punjab issue of 1985-95, insofar as it relates to the question of Sikh identity is self-explanatory. Therefore I do not intend to offer detailed comments or analysis. But still a few brief personal comments will be worthwhile.

The *first* major point which becomes very clear, particularly from the discussion in the Early Period (the detail of which is given in chapter 3) is that all the requirements needed for a separate identity are found in the works and teachings of the ten Sikh Gurus. The three most important events which took place during the first two centuries of Sikh history (1469-1708) require our special attention. *One*, the appointment of a successor of Guru

Nanak Devji became the basis for the continuity of the leadership for the future. *Two*, the compilation of the Sikh scripture by the fifth Guru Arjan Dev, which contained the most authentic teachings of the Gurus and other saints; this became the basis of Sikh ideology to guide the everyday lives of Sikh believers in the years to come. And *three*, a very important event was the founding of the Khalsa by the tenth Guru, Gobind Singh, based upon a set of very distinctive rules of discipline, which provided a visible clear-cut identity for the members of the Khalsa brotherhood. These factors based on the above three most important events of Sikh history in the years to come will save the Sikh religion from absorption into Hinduism[17] as well as help in sustaining the Sikh identity.

A *second* most important point which becomes clear from the discussion, is that particularly during the 'British Period' the identity question of the Sikh community became very crucial, and in sharpening it, the policies of the British rulers was very helpful. The policy of census and recruitment in the army were especially helpful in this matter. The Sikh movement during the British period ultimately culminated in the formation of various important Sikh institutions like the SGPC, followed by the organization of Akali Dal, a political arm of SGPC. Both SGPC and Akali Dal have led the Sikh masses towards establishing a separate Sikh identity.

The *third* important point becomes very clear, particularly from the discussion on the post-Independence era from 1947 till date that the Sikh struggle for a separate identity is still continuing, which of course is now mixed up with a number of other issues including religious, political, social and economic ones, but all these ultimately point towards a separate Sikh identity. Interestingly, if one goes carefully through the text of the various resolutions adopted by the Shiromani Akali Dal, at different times, including the ones referred to in our discussion, it becomes very clear that the notion of a separate state was never firmly demanded by the Akalis. On the other hand, if one goes through the language used by the government documents such as the *White Paper on the Punjabi Agitation*, one gets a very clear-cut interpretation which leads towards a definite notion of a separate state and other related issues, which at some stage, started appealing to some sections of the people and gave them the basis for their narrow struggle.

In the discussion in the post-independent era, the other point which becomes clear is from the text of the agreement which was signed by Rajiv Gandhi and Harcharan Singh Longowal, on 24 July 1985. In this agreement both sides have clearly agreed on the issues related to territory, sharing of river water and the centre-state relations, including greater autonomy to the states. Today, these three issues, particularly the last one, is the basis of conflict related to the Punjab issue, which, if taken in the right spirit, could have been solved easily.

The role of the media though in passing, is also crucial, either in aggravating or in reconciling the situation in the Punjab. If the media persons and their channels would follow the positive media ethics while giving their opinion or judgement on such issues, our problems will be far less. For example, the *Indian Express* reported faithfully the Amritsar resolution of the new United Akali Party dated 2 May 1994. But then on 3 May 1994, the same daily in a way helped in aggravating the issue by giving a very clearly one-sided judgement on this whole issue. This is where the role of the media becomes important in dealing with issues like that of the Punjab.

6. CONCLUDING REMARKS

In this chapter only glimpses of the decade-old Sikh struggle, which reached its height between 1985 and 1995 is given in order to show, how in our own time, the threat to Sikh identity continued and which the Sikh community is continuing to face. This process is still on and is also important for a living community and is for her strength. In the discussion in the subsequent chapters, we will see how the Sikh community's identity is becoming more and more visible through her practising spirituality, charity and her role in the whole area of inter-religious dialogue.

NOTES

1. Madanji Kapur (ed.), *Co-Existence in Pluralistic Society: Punjab Issues and Prospects*, Amritsar, 1991, p. 187.
2. Pranay Gupte, *India: The Challenge of Change*, London, 1989, p. 128.
3. John C.B. Webster, *The Dalit Christian: A History*, Delhi, 1992, pp. 77, 78.
4. Rajiv A. Kapur, *Sikh Separatism: The Politics of Faith*, London, 1986, pp. 12, 14, 131.
5. Ibid., p. 15.
6. Ibid., pp. 10, 26.
7. Ibid., p. 22.
8. Ibid., p. 187.
9. See for detailed discussion, ibid., pp. 190-1, 206-7.
10. James Massey (ed.), *Indigenous People, Dalits (Dalit Issues in Today's Theological Debate)*, Delhi, 1994, pp. 38-40.
11. Marc Galanter, *Competing Equalities*, Delhi, 1984, p. 144.
12. Gupte, op. cit., pp. 131-2.
13. Ghani Jafar, *The Sikh Volcano*, Lahore, 1987, p. 465.
14. Ibid., pp. 668-70.
15. Ibid., pp. 471-2.
16. A.S. Narang, *Punjab Politics in National Perspective*, Delhi, 1988, pp. 208-11.
17. Prakash Tandon, *Punjabi Saga (1857-1982)*, Delhi, 1988, pp. 658-61.

Part Three

SPECIFIC THEMES

5

Guru Nanak Devji's Concept of Creation

1. INTRODUCTION

At the outset of this chapter, one important point which needs to be mentioned is that Guru Nanak Devji's concern in his hymns is not to state a systematic self-concept of a creator and his creation, because basically he is a religious mystic. His hymns arose out of various personal human conditions, including his discussion on the concept of the Creator, creation and the relationship between the two. The basic question relating to universal human need, has been stated by Guru Nanakji in *Japu Sahib*.

Kiv saciārā hoiai, Kiv Kuṛai tutai pāli.
Hukami rajāī calanā Nānak likhiā nāli.
Hukami horani ākāru hukamu na Kahia jāi.

How can one be true, how can the veil of false illusion be torn?
Nanak, it is by obeying His will according to His order,
which is already written in our being.
By His order the creation came into being,
But His order cannot be described.[1]

This part of the opening stanza of *Japu Sahib* as well as the *Sri Guru Granth Sahib*, tell us about the basic concern of Guru Nanak Devji, which he has raised in the form of a question: How can a human being be truthful?[2] And how can the veil of falsehood, which separates the human beings from the Ultimate Reality, be removed? The answer according to Guru Nanak Devji is by carrying out His Order, Will or Command, which is ordained. Here one needs to take note of His Order, i.e. *hukam*, because this again is repeated in the next stanza, as quoted above, in which *hukam* is the agent of creation. *Hukam* here is a link between the Ultimate Reality (which is *karata* as per the *Mul Mantr* and *akaru* (creation, which includes human beings). Reference will be made to this hymn again later in this chapter, but here the point which needs to be made clear is that Guru Nanak's starting point is a personal concern or need and that can be accomplished only by what originally was responsible for creation of human beings, i.e. *hukam*.

So in a way the reference which one finds is either briefly in the form of verses or they are in the form of long hymns describing the process of creation, which have been used by Guru Nanak Devji to narrate even greater concerns. But by doing so Guru Nanak Devji has given much matter in his hymns, which reveals both the nature of the Creator and His creation and also their relationship. In the next section an analysis is being made of Guru Nanak Devji's 'creation hymns'.

2. MAIN CREATION HYMNS AND THEIR ANALYSIS

2.1 *Hymns*

(i) *Arabada narabada dhundhūkārā.*
Dharṇi na gaganā hukamu apārā.
Na dinu raini na candu na suraju suna samadi lagāida . . .
Brahamā Bisanu Mahesu na koī.
Avaru na diasal iko soi . . .
Na Koi akhi vakhānai dūjā.

Āpe āpi upai vigasai ape kimati pāidā . . .
Na tadi Gorakhu na macchindo . . .
Bada Kateba na simmriti sāsāta. . . .
Kahatā bakata āpe agocaru āpe alakhu Iakhāida. . .
Ja tisu bhānā ta jagatu upāia.
Bājhu Kalā ādāṇu rahāiā.
Brahama Bisanu Mahesa upae māiā mohu vadhāida.
Virale ku guri sabadu sunaia kari kari dekhai hukamu sabāiā.
Khand Brahamand pātāl arambhe gupatahu
paragatī aidā.

Millions and trillions of years ago there was
only Impenetrable (*Dhundhukara*),
Invisible Transcendence.
There was neither earth nor sky.
(Only) Infinite (Being's) Will was there.
There was no day, no night, no moon, no sun,
(i.e., there was no time, space or movement).
(Only He) was there in absolute state of stillness or transcendence. . . .
There was no Brahma, Vishnu or Shiva.
Except the One, no one else was seen there. . . .
There was no talk or mention of the second (duality).
He (Lord) rejoiced by giving expression to Himself,
and He alone evaluated Himself. . . .
There was no Gorakh nor Machhindra. . . .
There were neither Vedas, nor Semetic Books, nor
Simirtis nor Oriental Shastras.
The (Lord) Himself was speaker and preacher,
He, the Imperceptible and Unseen, Himself saw everything.
When He willed, He made the world,
and without any support stretched the vast expanse.
He made Brahma, Vishnu and Shiva.
Also he created Maya (multifariousness and attraction among the created).
To a rare one He imparted the Word.
He made the creation and watches it,
And his Order ran through the Universe.
He divided the Universe into continents and under worlds.
Thus from the Transcendent and the Mysterious He made the Visible or the Manifest.[3]

(ii) *Sunna Kalā aparampari dhārī.*
Āpi niralāmu apara apārī
Ape Kudarati Kari Kari dekhu sunnhu
sunnu upāidā.
Paunu pānī sunnai te sāje.
Sirasathi upāi Kāiā gara raje . . .
Sunnhu Brahama Bisanu Mahesu upāe.
Sunne Varate juga sabāe . . .
Sunnhu candu suraju gainare.
Tis Kī joti tirabhavan sāre.
Sunne alakha apara niralamu
sunne tārī lāida.
Sunnhu dharati akasu upāe.
Binu thammā rakhe sacu Kalapāe.
Tirabhavan sāji mekhulī maiā api upāē
Khapāida . . .
Sunnhu upajī sunni samānī.
Utabhuju calatu Kīā siri Karatai
bisamadu sabadi dekhāidā . . .
Ape Karanu Kia aparampari sabhu
tero Kīā Kamāida.

The illimitable Lord in the unattributed state
of perfect stillness (*sunna*), assumed His might,
Himself remaining unattached/separate and boundless.
Himself He brings about the creation,
and watches it creating from this state
substances devoid of consciousness.
From this unattributed state were created air and water.
Raising creation, in citadel of the body is He situated as Monarch.
From the unattributed state were raised Brahma, Vishnu and Shiva.
In all ages was this unattributed state pervasive.
Sun, moon and the sky appeared from this state of *sunna.*
And it is His light that pervades the three worlds.
In unbroken trance abides the Lord unknowable,
limitless and unattached, fallen into trance in the *sunna.*
From the *sunna* were created earth and sky,
sustained without pillars by power of truth.
Creating the three worlds, by the string of *Maya*[4] are these
bound. . .
Himself these He creates and destroys.

From the *sunna* arisen, into the *sunna* are these absorbed:
The Creator has displayed the marvel of creation;
and through His Word, made the miracle manifest.
Himself the Lord beyond limit created causation
All act as per His Will.[5]

(iii) *Ape sacu Kia Kāra Jori.*
Aṇḍaja phoṛi jori vichori
Dharati akāsu Kīe baisana Ku thāu;
Rati dinantu Kīe bhau bhau.
Jini Kīe Kari Vekhanhare . . .
Avaru nā dūjā sirajanahārā.

Himself made (the creation) by joining (all).
By breaking the Egg *andaja* He joined and unjoined them.*
He made the earth and sky places to live (Space).
He made night and day (time and motion) and fear and love.
He made the creation, also takes care of it.
None other than He is Creator.[6]

2.2 *Analysis*

The three hymns quoted above agree on most details except the beginning of creation, which is a very important factor for understanding both the nature of the Creator and creation. Therefore, these need a systematic analysis, which is being conducted under the following three heads:

- *Dhundhukara* (Deep Darkness)
- *Sunnu* (Dormancy)
- *Andaja* (Egg)

These three phrases also echo the three creation concepts, which belong to the earlier religious traditions of India and will also be referred to in our discussion.

* *Andaja* does not mean an egg, but creation or entire life originating from an egg. Thus, a more accurate translation of the verse would be, 'The True Lord with His hands (or Himself) created life. He also destroys it, creates again and destroys it and continues the cycle: He created Earth and Sky for dwelling. He also made day and night and invested the creation with fear and love.'

2.2.1 DHUNDHUKARA

This *dhundhukara* creation hymn is the most popular and is referred to so the hymn of Guru Nanak Devji. Almost all scholars, who have in some form dealt with this concept of Guru Nanak, have made reference to this hymn.[7] A similar hymn is also found in the *Rigveda*,[8] and scholars have referred to that hymn as a basis to describe creation 'out of nothing'.[9] As per the *Puratan Janam Sakhi*,[10] Guru Nanak Devji composed this hymn during his third journey (CE 1515-17) in which he visited Kashmir.

This *dhundhukara* hymn has sixteen long verses. In verse one Guru Nanak has made references to the pre-creation state and Infinite Lord's state of that time. In verses 2 and 3 a general description of the *sunna* state (unattributed state of perfect stillness) and creation has been given. Verses 4, 6, 7, 8, 10 and 13 describe the non-existence of various Hindu gods, religious practices, scriptures, etc. The same way verses 5 and 9 talk about the Sant and Nath traditions, including the non-existence of their leaders Gorakh and Machhindra. In verses 11 and 13 Guru Nanak talks about the non-existence of the Muslim religious practices, scriptures, etc., and in verse 12 again the description of the non-existence of the general human relationships in the beginning has been given.

In these first 13 verses, Guru Nanak Devji has made two very important points: First, that there was a state of non-existence of the world and what is seen in it. The whole negative description refers to this very fact. Second, the existence of the infinite, imperceptible and unseen (Lord or Being) and His Will (*Hukamu*) is affirmed in verse 1 and the last part of verse 13. The overall stress seen here is on the absoluteness or absolute nature of the Creator.

In the second part of the *dhundhukara* hymn (verses 14, 15 and 16), Guru Nanak Devji describes how creation took place. The first thing he makes clear is the reason behind creation. He says, it is because of the 'Will' (*bhana*) of the Creator. Then in verses 14 and 15, he gives a clear description of how the Creator made the whole world including His forces of creation, sustenance, and destruction (symbolized as three main gods, i.e.

Brahma, Vishnu and Shiva respectively). In verse 16, Guru Nanak Devji says that he has received this knowledge from the Perfect Teacher.

The most important point, or the summary of this hymn, is found in the last part of verse 15: *gupatahu paragati aida*, i.e. 'from the unmanifest, He became manifest'. Through the act of creation the Creator Lord (who is absolute in His nature, but imperceptible and unseen) made Himself known. So here we find through His *bhana*, i.e. 'Will' and in His follow-up act of creation, the revelation of His nature through His created world.

The last point to be examined about the *dhundhukara* hymn is the phrase *dhundhukara* itself. These have been translated variously as 'chaos' (by Gopal Singh),[11] 'utter darkness' (by Man Mohan Singh),[12] and 'darkness' (by Talib).[13] In Panjabi language the meaning of its root, *dhund*, is mist.[14] Therefore, the literal meaning can be 'mistiness'. These literal meanings, of course, raise the question whether 'darkness', 'mistiness' or even 'chaos', was already existing or was also created.[15]

The important point which needs to be remembered is that through the phrase *dhundhukara*, Guru Nanak Devji has tried to describe the pre-creation state.

2.2.2 SUNNU

The second hymn quoted above is being addressed as the *sunnu* hymn of the creation. This hymn is also long, having 16 verses spread out on two pages of the *Sri Guru Granth Sahib* (pp. 1037, 1038). From the content as well as the main term used in the hymn, and also after comparing it with the language and content of Guru Nanak Devji's other writings like Sidha Gosati, particularly verses 50 and 51, it becomes clear that this hymn is addressed to a person or persons, with a Buddhist background.[16] One such known group, whom Guru Nanak Devji came into contact with, was of Sant and Nathas religious groups who shared the Buddhist religious thoughts.* According to G.S. Khosla, Guru

* Naths are Saivites.

Nanak Devji used this hymn while having a dialogue with a Lama.[17]

This hymn does not present any views about the pre-creation state, except that in verse 1 Guru Nanak Devji states the Absolute (*aparampari*) nature of the Creator, who is not only infinite (*apari*), but also unique and different (*niralamu apara*). The point which needs to be noted is that He is not the same as His creation, or He is not identical with it. This is the impression one gets from his hymn, particularly from the verses like 'From the unattributed void they came into existence and into the same they will merge'. In verse 10 Guru Nanak Devji makes it clear: 'The Absolute (*aparampari*) Lord Himself caused (*karanu*) it all'. Again, the Creator's infinite and unique (*apara niralamu*) nature is stressed. These thoughts of Guru Nanak Devji make it very clear how his concept of creation is opposed to the pantheistic view.

As mentioned earlier, he created beings' list given in the *sunnu* hymn is very similar to the *dhundhukara* hymn, so some of the general discussion on the content of this hymn need not be taken up. But the important point of discussion here is the phrase *sunnu* itself. Various translations of the *Sri Guru Granth Sahib* do not agree on its meaning. For example, Gopal Singh has translated it as 'Absolute Self',[18] and very close to him is Man Mohan Singh's rendering of it as 'the Absolute Lord'.[19] The most recent translation is of Talib, who translated *sunnu* as 'void'.[20] Our above rendering is also close to Talib's.*

Sunnu (void) or *sunyavadu* (voidness of appearance is a well-known concept) and has a Buddhist background. Mahayana, one of the major sects of Buddhism believed in it, and its thinker Nagarjuna (author of *Illusion Theory*) expounded it. This concept rejects all theories of causality. They believe that cause and effect are identical. According to them

> . . . causal changes are just a transformation of a single underlying substance. . . . All empirical phenomena are insubstantial and relative, yet their inner nature can be said to be constituted by Voidness. Thus

* *Sunnu* here means nothing except the eternal Lord Himself who always existed.

the world is seen from the standpoint of discursive reason, and perception is unreal, and in its place one must substitute an apprehension of the Void. This, admittedly very thinly described, functions in the systems as sort of the Absolute. Thus, the Void or 'Suchness' (as it is sometimes referred to) is, in effect, in the Ultimate Reality.[21]

On the basis of the above comment one can say without doubt that Void probably refers to the Absolute and this thought may have influenced some of the translators and commentators who have translated *sunnu* as 'Absolute Lord or Self'. For example, in the translation of Gopal Singh the creation acts begin with this phrase 'out of His Absolute Self came . . .', and similar is the pattern of Man Mohan Singh, i.e.

From the Absolute Lord issued (or came). . . . This is where the creation concept of emanation comes in as also the concept of Monism. But, as mentioned already, Guru Nanak Devji has made it very clear in verses 1, 10 and 15 how the Creator is unique and separate, because He Himself is the cause of all that we see in this world. In fact, in verse 7 he has used the term *Karatai* (Creator) and said, 'The Creator made and displayed the creation (*untabhuja*)'.

We will discuss later how the Void concept, which makes this world insubstantial and unreal, is not applicable to the views of Guru Nanak Devji.

2.2.3 ANDAJA

Unlike the earlier two creations, i.e. *dhundhukara* and *sunnu* hymns, there is less problem with the translation of this hymn, except in the case of Man Mohan Singh, who has rendered *andaja* as 'spheres'[22] without much support. It seems he has taken *andaja's* shape as round or circular and has translated it as a sphere. Though there is a Punjabi phrase, *mandala*, which means sphere or circle.[23] Anyhow, the meaning of *andaja* is very clear, i.e. egg and even Guru Nanak Devji has used the same word in another hymn, where he says:*

* As per earlier note *andaja* does not mean egg. It includes all life.

Andaja jaraja utabhuja setaja terẹ kite janta.
Those born from egg, placenta, earth or sweat are all your creation.[24]

The authoritative Punjabi source gives the meaning of *andaja* as egg.[25] The details of the created world, in this hymn, again agree with the other two creation hymns. But this is not an independent hymn, but is part of a longer work or poem written by Guru Nanak Devji in Raga Bilavalu. Guru Nanak Devji has used 15 lunar days to say the whole poem. On the first lunar day he gives the description of the Absolute Being who is, according to him, One, but unique (*nirala*), eternal, without birth, without identity, without impurity, inaccessible, inscrutable, without form, but pervades in every human heart. On the second lunar day he describes the basic problems a human being faces, i.e. death, lust, etc. On the third and fourth days he narrates the creation story. On the remaining lunar days 5-15, Guru Nanak Devji gives other instructions.

He begins with the Creator's initiative for creation (ape, i.e. Himself). The creation list, like the other two hymns of Guru Nanak Devji, includes earth, sky, night, day, gods and goddesses including Brahma, Vishnu, Shiva, Vedas, Puranas, Shastras, etc. This hymn makes two points very clear: that the Creator not only made all, but also takes care of all (*vekhanharu*), and that there is only one Creator, whom he addresses on the first lunar day as *ekamkaru*, i.e. One Absolute Being. The phrase used to say this fact is the most powerful *avaru na duja sirajanahara*, i.e. (of the creation) there is no other (second) Creator except Him.

The problem in this hymn is with the use of the word *andaja*, i.e. egg. If one takes the meaning of *andaja phori Jon vichori* to be 'by breaking the egg He joined and unjoined' the implication of 'egg' here is that the Creator is making His creation from a pre-existing matter.* The same question arose about *dhundhukara*

* As already pointed out, we do not subscribe to this interpretation. *Andaja* refers to the entire life. Moreover, Guru Nanak Devji naturally refers to existing concepts as symbols to make himself understandable, but his meanings are entirely his own and quite often different from, or even contrary to, the old concepts.

(deep darkness). Here the act of creation is directly related to 'egg'. Also there is echo of the already existing concept of creation based on *Hiranyagarbha*, i.e. golden egg.[26] According to this concept, first the Creator Lord arose from a golden egg and then He created all. According to Manu, this *Hiranyagarbha* is the name of Brahma, who took birth in the golden egg and for one year lived in this egg. While Brahma was still in the egg as per his wish he broke the egg of which one part became heaven and other earth.[27]

While going through the content of Guru Nanak Devji's hymns, it becomes clear that his phrases and names are according to context or people he met. The earlier two hymns, have been spoken to different groups. This argument is applicable here also. Guru Nanak Devji has used the symbol of *andaja* (egg) to express his thoughts about the creation. Here, as already mentioned, his stress is on the One Lord as Creator. In this he has again stressed that all gods and goddesses including Brahma, Vishnu and Shiva, are part of the created world. The question of creating from pre-existing matter (egg) has not been answered in this hymn. Partly, it might be that it is not an independent hymn. It is part of a longer poem, in which many other basic thoughts and teachings have been dealt with. But the problem of pre-existing matter has been very clear and has been dealt with in Guru Nanak's other hymns, especially in the first creation hymn, which we have named as *dhundukara*.

3. MORE REFERENCES TO THE CREATOR AND CREATION

Before concluding this paper, it will be worthwhile to examine some of the selected references concerning both the Creator and creation in Guru Nanak Devji's other hymns. Some of these will throw further light on the various aspects of the creation concept of Guru Nanak Devji. For example, how, why and when the creation was created. Is this creation eternal or false? Who supports or keeps it going? In this section we examine these questions.

3.1 *How Creation was Created?*

Guru Nanak Devji answers this question in Japu twice. He says:

Hukami hovani akaru.[28]

By His order the creation (forms) came into being.

Again Guru Nanak Devji says:

Kita pasau iko Kavau.[29]

He made the world's expanse with one saying.

In Dakhani Omkaru Guru Nanak Devji says:

Omkari Brahama utpati[30]

Omkari created Brahma.

Here in these references *Kavau* and *Omkari* refer to *sabad* (word) as agent of Creation. *Hukam* also refers to the same reality. Order is expressed through the use of word or words. Therefore word is the agent, which the Creator used to make this world.

3.2 *When was Creation Created?*

Guru Nanak Devji himself has raised this question in Japu. He says:

Kavanu su vela vakhatu Kavanu kavan thiti Kavanu varu.
Kavani si ruti mahu Kavanu jitu hoa akaru. [31]

What was the time or moment, and what was the date or day,
What was the season or month, When the creation was made?
Or when forms came into being?

At the same place in Japu, Guru Nanak has also given an answer to this question. But before giving the answer he says, Pandits cannot answer this question on the basis of their knowledge of Purana's texts, nor the Qazis from the Quran. Even Naths cannot tell the day, season or month, when the creation was made. Guru Nanak's answer is:

Ja karata sirathi Ku safe
Ape jansi soi.[32]

The Creator who fashioned the creation,
He only knows the time (of creation).

3.3. *Why was Creation Created?*

Guru Nanak's answer to this question is as follows:

Gurumukhi dharati saja.[33]

It is for the God-conscious that He has fashioned this earth.

In another place Guru Nanak says:

Dharati upai dhari dharamasala.[34]

He made this earth as a place of practising righteousness.

Guru Nanak also said that the human beings are created to serve the Creator:

Phuramani hai Kar Khasami pathaia.[35]

The Master has sent the human being into this world with an order to serve Him.

So one of the purposes of this world is that the Creator wants human beings to live and practise righteousness. This thought is expressed in the *andaja* hymn also: *baisana ku thau* (place to live).

3.4. *Is this Creation Unreal?*

Guru Nanak Devji says:

Nanak sace ki saci kara.[36]

O Nanak, True is creation of the True One.

In *Vara Asa* Guru Nanak again says:

sace tere Khand sace brahamand;
Sace tere loa sace akar.[37]

True are your continents and true are your firmaments,
True are your worlds and true are your creation (forms).

These references do not need any explanation because these are self-explanatory. Everything the Creator has created is real and true.

3.5. *Is this Creation eternal?*

The Guru says:

Dhahi usare dhare dhianu.[38]

He destroys, and makes, keeping all ever in mind.

The above reference makes it clear that this creation is not eternal. The Creator created this many times and also destroyed the same. There are a number of hymns, where Guru Nanak Devji makes it clear that except the Creator Himself, nothing in this world is eternal. For example:

(a) *Aasathiru Karata dekhiai horu Keti avai jai.*

The creator is the only one seen as stable; all others continue coming and going.

(b) *Sabha duni avanu javani mukamu Iku rahimu.*[40]

The whole world is subject to coming and going.
One merciful Lord is permanent.

3.6. *What is the Extent of the Creation?*

Guru Nanak Devji in Raga Asa has raised the question of the extent of the creation in these words:

Nali Kutambu sathi varadata Brahama bhalan sirasti gaia.
Agai antu na paio.[41]

Brahma the giver of boons with his family members went to find (the extent) of the creation; but even going further and further, he could not find the end.

In Japu Guru Nanak Devji gives his view about the extent of the creation:

Anta na japai para varu.[42]

It seems there is no limit of His created creation.

For, it is equal to the Name of the Creator about which Guru Nanak Devji says:

Jeta Kita teta nau.

As Your creation is great, so is your Name.

3.7. *Who Takes Care of the Creation?*

In a number of hymns Guru Nanak tells that the Creator Himself provides the needs and takes care of His creation. Examples:

(a) *Nanak jant upai Kai samule subhanaha.*[44]

O Nanak, after making all the beings,
He himself takes care of them all.

(b) *So Karata Kadar Karimu de*
jiai rijak samabahi.[45]

The Creator, who is Almighty and Gracious, gives food to all.

(c) *Ape Satigaru ape sevaku*
ape sirathi upai he.[46]

He Himself is the True Guru, and the Servant, and He Himself made the creation.

4. CONCLUDING REMARKS

From the overall discussion in this essay on various creation hymns and references, two aspects of the nature of the Creator (who is Ik Omkar), become clear, i.e. the absolute (unmanifested) and the personal (manifested). These two are summed up in the phrase of *dhundukara* hymn, i.e. *guptahu pargat aida* (from the unmanifested He becomes manifested). Also the same thought is found in *sunnu* hymn, i.e. *sunnu upaji* (from the unattributed Void they come into existence). *Andaja* hymn affirms the creative personal aspect of *sirajanahar*, i.e. Creator. The key phrases *dhundhukara* and *sunnu* refer to the pre-creation state.

The question of creation coming out of 'nothing', or 'pre-existent matter', or 'Out of Creator', is not the basic subject of the creation hymns of Guru Nanak Devji. His basic subject is the sovereignty of the Creator over His Creation. At the same time distinction between the Creator and creation has been maintained in the hymns. Phrases like *niralamu* (different), *apara* (boundless), *nirala* (unique), etc., show clearly that the Creator is above His creation. The discussion under the head, 'More references to Creator and Creation' again establishes the fact of the Creator's lordship and eternity. Also the personal aspect of the Creator's nature becomes further evident in this section to which phrases like *samale* (takes care) and *de . . . rijak* (gives food) are the pointers.

The last, but an important point becomes clear, that all human beings (without any hierchical difference based upon occupation as is the case with caste-based human social order), are sent in this world to serve Him and to practise righteousness upon the earth (section 3.3).

NOTES

1. *SGGS*, p. 1.
2. Teja Singh, *Japji*, Amritsar, 1974, p. 19.
3. *SGGS*, pp. 1035-6.
4. *Maya* here means worldly delights, which appear as real, but is actually corrupting (C.A. Shackle, *Guru Nanak Glossary*, London, 1981, p. 237).
5. *SGGS*, pp. 1037-8.
6. *AG*, p. 839.
7. Sunil Kumar Das, *Sri Caitanaya and Guru Nanak*, Calcutta, 1985, pp. 124-5; Anil Chandra Banerjee, *Guru Nanak and His Times*, Patiala, 1984, pp. 153-4; Sher Singh, *Philosophy of Sikhism*, Amritsar, 1986, p. 180; Surinder Singh Kohli, *Philosophy of Guru Nanak*, Chandigarh, 1976, pp. 80, 81; B.S. Khosla, 'Guru Nanak's Conception of the Origin of the Universe', in *Guru Nanak: A Homage*, ed. K.R. Srinivasa Iyenger, Delhi, 1973, pp. 110-11; Wazir Singh 'The Sikh Cosmology', in *Journal of Sikh Studies*, vol VI, no. 2, 2 August 1979, p. 73.
8. Quoted in *A History of Indian Philosophy* by Surendranath Dasgupta, vol. 1, Delhi, 1988 (rpt.), p. 24.
9. Maurice Phillips, *The Teaching of the Vedas*, Delhi, 1976 (rpt.), p. 114.

10. Bhai Vir Singh, *Puratana Janam Sakhi Sri Guru Nanak Devji*, Amritsar, 1971, p. 172.
11. Gopal Singh, *Sri Guru Granth Sahib* (English version), Chandigarh, vol. 4, 1978, p. 983.
12. Man Mohan Singh, *Sri Guru Granth Sahib* (English and Punjabi translation), Amritsar, vol. 6, 1964, p. 3396.
13. Gurbachan Singh Talib (tr.), *Sri Guru Granth Sahib* (English translation), Patiala, vol. 2, 1985, p. 2114.
14. *Punjabi Kosha*, Patiala, 1967, vol. III, pp. 510, 511.
15. Phillips, op. cit., p. 119.
16. *AG*, p. 943.
17. Khosla, op. cit., p. 115.
18. Gopal Singh, vol. 4, p. 990.
19. Man Mohan Singh, vol. 6, p. 2119.
20. Talib, vol. 2, p. 2119.
21. Ninian Smart, *Doctrine and Argument in Indian Philosophy*, London, 1964, pp. 54-5.
22. Man Mohan Singh, vol. 5, p. 2732.
23. *Punjabi Kosha*, vol. 5, 'Mandala', p. 66.
24. *AG*, p. 596.
25. S.V., Kahan Singh, *Gurusabada Ratanakara Mahan Kosh*, 'Andaj', p. 113.
26. Phillips, op. cit., pp. 122-32.
27. Kahan Singh, p. 276.
28. *SGGS*, p. 1.
29. Ibid., p. 3.
30. Ibid., p. 929.
31. Ibid., p. 7.
32. Ibid., p. 7.
33. Ibid., p. 941.
34. Ibid., p. 1033.
35. Ibid., p. 142.
36. Ibid., p. 7.
37. Ibid., p. 463.
38. Ibid., p. 354.
39. Ibid., p. 54.
40. Ibid., p. 64.
41. Ibid., p. 350.
42. Ibid., p. 5.
43. Ibid., p. 5.
44. Ibid., p. 466.
45. Ibid., p. 474.
46. Ibid., p. 1026.

6

Spirituality

1. CASE HISTORIES

1.1. *Guru Nanak at Sultanpur*

In the early years of Guru Nanak Devji's spiritual journey, he was working as an in-charge of the treasury of Daulat Khan Lodi at Sultanpur (now in Kapurthala district, Punjab). According to Guru Nanak Devji's daily practice, one day, early morning, he along with his servant went for a bath in a nearby river. He took off his clothes and after giving these to his servant, he entered the water. His servant waited for some time for the return of Guru Nanak Devji, but even after some hours he did not return. Therefore he went to the town and told the whole incident to Khan. Khan along with others went to the river and tried to search for Guru Nanak Devji in the water. But when they could not find him, they returned to the town and were very sad.

But then after three days Guruji suddenly appeared and when people met him, the first words he which he uttered was

Na ko Hindu na Musalman

There is neither Hindu nor Muslim.[1]

1.2. *Guru Nanak Devji at Hardwar*

After Guru Nanak Devji's spiritual vision at Sultanpur, he undertook a number of journeys all over India. He even travelled to Sri Lanka, Nepal, Tibet, Mecca and Bangladesh, with his message of peace and reconciliation, i.e. 'There is neither Hindu nor Muslim'. During one of his sojourns, Guru Nanak Devji went to Hardwar, where he saw that the (people), while taking bath in the sacred Ganges river, were throwing water towards the rising sun (east) as an offering to their dead ancestors. Guru Nanak Devji stood near them and started throwing water in the opposite direction (west). When the other devotees questioned him about what he was doing, he replied calmly, 'I am watering my fields near Lahore in Punjab.' The people laughed at him and said, 'How can this water reach your fields near Lahore?' Guru Nanak Devji replied to them, 'If your water can reach your dead ancestors in heaven, which according to you is 49,00,00,000 miles ending from here, then surely my water will also reach there.' The people understood Guru Nanak Devji's message.[2]

1.3. *Guru Nanak Devji at Mecca*

At another time Guru Nanak Devji went to Mecca. While staying at Mecca, one day he slept with his feet towards Kaaba. When other pilgrims saw Guru Nanak Devji sleeping in that state, one of them came and told him, 'By keeping your feet towards Kaaba, you are showing disrespect to this holy place.' Guru Nanak Devji immediately replied to him, 'If you feel I am showing disrespect by having my feet towards the holy place, in that case you may please turn my feet in some other direction, where God does not dwell.' So a Muslim pilgrim tried to move Guru Nanak Devji's feet to the other direction and was amazed to see the Kaaba also moving in the same direction.[3]

The above three instances are taken from the *Janamsakhis* of Guru Nanak Devji. (The *Janamsakhis* literally means the testimonial stories related to the life of Guru Nanak Devji.) These three case histories very clearly explain the kind of spiritualities that were being practised at the time of Guru Nanak Devji and how he dealt with them. Guru Nanak Devji was the founder Guru of Sikh religion. Therefore as a founder Guru, whatever content of Sikh religion including the spirituality he laid down, still remains the same. But it is also true that his successors, the other nine Gurus, further expanded his teaching, which later on were canonized under the leadership and guidance of the fifth Guru Arjan Devji and the tenth Guru Gobind Singhji, with a final title *Sri Guru Granth Sahib* (the shorter title of which is commonly known as *Adi Granth*).[4]

Here, because of limitation of space, it will not be possible to deal with the history of the development of Sikh religion's teaching on 'spirituality', instead we will limit our discussion, *first* to the historical religious and cultural context in which the Sikh spirituality was born and *second* we will have a brief discussion on the actual 'Sikh spirituality' with special reference to its founder Guru Nanak Devji's teaching.

2. THE HISTORICAL, RELIGIOUS AND CULTURAL CONTEXT

It is true that the spirituality of any community is always the outcome of the historical experience of the members of the community in which they are placed. It also means that every spirituality is contextual in nature, because it is the historical context (including cultural, religion social, political and economic), which contribute to the formation of a spirituality. This is exactly what we find in the background of Sikh spirituality. For example, the religious life of people in Guru Nanak Devji's time was in a most degrading state. The followers of both the religions, Hinduism and Islam, had become most corrupted and degraded. Everything in the religious spheres which followed only helped the religious leaders. The caste system had different sub-castes. From Guru Nanak Devji's hymns it appears that all the religious positions had become hereditary. This state of affairs we see very clear in the following hymns of Guru Nanak Devji for which with the original text and, the translation of S. Manmohan Singh is given below:

Hindū kai ghari hindū āvai. Sūtu janeū paṛi gali pāvai.
Sūtu pāi kare buriāī. Nātā dhotā thāi na pāī.
Muslamānu kare vadaāī. Viṇu gura pīrai ko thāi na pāī.
Rāhu dasāi othai ko jāī. Karaṇī bājhu bhiṣti na pāī.
Jogī kai ghari jugti dasāī. Titu kārṇī kani mundrā pāī.
Mundrā pāi phirai sansāri. Jithai kithai sirjṇahāru.
Jete jīa tete vātāū. Cīrī āī dila na kāū.
Ethai jāṇai su jāe sinnāṇai. Horu phakaṛu Hindū Musalmānai.
Sabhanā kā dari lekhā hoi. Karaṇī bājhahu tarai na koi.
Sacu sacu vakhāṇai koi. Nānak agai pucha na hoi.

The Hindu comes to the house of the Hindu
Chanting the sermon, he puts on the yarn sacred thread on the boy's neck.
Putting on the tread, he commits sins.
For his ablutions and washings he is approved not.
The Muslim praises his faith.
Without the Guru and the Divine teacher, none is accepted.
Even when the way is pointed out rare is the one who reaches there.
Without good deeds, heaven is attained not.
One goes to the Yogi's monastery to ask the way to God.
For that purpose, he puts rings in his ears.
With earrings on, he wanders about the world.
He realises not, the Creator-Lord is everywhere. As many as are the beings, so many are the travellers.
When the death warrant comes, none can make any delay.
He, who knows the Lord here, recognises Him in that place.
Other, whether Hindus or Muslims are but praters.
All mortals' accounts are taken in the Lord's court and none is saved without good deeds.
He who utters the Name of the Truest of the true, O Nanak, is not called to account, hereafter.

About the general moral and political condition of his time, Guru Nanak Devji in one of his others hymns says:

Kali katī kasaī dharamu
pankh kari udariā . . .

The age is like a dragon sword
The kings are butchers;
Goodness has taken wings and flown

When the Mughal invader Babur attacked India and created terrible distruction, on that Guru Nanak Devji, somewhat like an Old Testament prophet, could not control himself and cried out loud to God in these words:

Khurasana Khasamana kia hindusatanu daraia.
Apai dosu na dei karata jamu kari mugalu craia.
Eti maya pai kuralane tain ki daradu na aia.

Though Khurashan has been shielded by thee.
Though terror has struck at the heart,
Thou, O Creator of all things,
Takes hath sent *Yama*, disguised as the great Moghul Babur.
Terrible was the slaughter,
Loud were cries of the lamenters.
Did this not awaken pity in thee, O Lord?
Thou are and parcel of all things equally, O Creator:
Thou must feel for all men and all nations.[5]

If one reads these hymns of Guru Nanak Devji along with the three case histories listed in the beginning of this chapter, one can easily understand how the spirituality of Guru Nanak was rooted in the historical, religious and cultural context of his times. Guru Nanak's spirituality (which is the foundation of Sikh spirituality), is a cry for human equality and divine justice.

3. SIKH SPIRITUALITY

In a way Guru Nanak Devji's teaching, which we find in his hymns found in *Sri Guru Granth Sahib* are the outcome of his spiritual experiences and his direct encounter with God (the Ultimate Reality). Basically Guru Nanak Devji was a religious person who cannot be brought under the category of a systemic theologian, because he was not concerned with providing rational answers to the various questions of human life.[6] These two points became very clear from the three case histories given in the beginning of this chapter. Beginning with his first direct encounter with the Ultimate Reality at Sultanpur and later examples of Hardwar and Mecca, tell us how this spiritual vision of God and his relationship will this world, particularly with human beings, became clearer and clearer. In one of his hymns, he tells his disciples Lalo, how he receives the divine message and how he delivers the same to others. Guru Nanak Devji says:

Jaioi mai avai khasama ki bani
Taisra kari gianh ve Lalo

As the word of the Lord comes to me
The same I let others know, O Lalo.[7]

The other important point which we need to remember is that Guru Nanak Devji's basic concern in life was the human need, which he expressed at the beginning of his most important work *Japuji Sahib* (the first book of the *Adi Granth*), in the form of a question:

Kiva saciara hoia
Kirva kurai tutai pali.

How can one be true,
How can the veil of false illusion be torn?

This was the question with which Guru Nanak was engaged throughout his life, because this question in real sense is related to a universal human need. Guru Nanak of course based upon his personal spiritual experience, found an answer to the above question, about which he says:

Hukami rajai calana,
Nanak likhia nali.

Nanak, it is by obeying His will,
According to His order (command),
Which is already written in our being.[8]

In *Japuji Sahib* of course before raising the above question and also answering the same, Guru Nanak Devji also rejected the existing spiritualities by saying:

Socai soci na hovaī je socī lakh vār.
Cupai cup na hovai je lāe rahā liv tār.
Bhukhiā bhukh na utrī je bannā puriā bhār.
Sahas siaṇpā lakh hohi ta ik na calai nāli.

By pondering on God, man cannot
Have a conception of him,
Even through he may ponder over lacs of times.

Even though one be silent
And remain absorbed in the Lord's constant love,
He obtains not be mind's silence.

The hunger of the hungry departs not,
even though they may pile up loads of the world's valuables.

Man may possess thousands and lacs of wits,
but not even one (avails him in the Lord's court) or (goes with him).[9]

Here in this hymn, Guru Nanak Devji has very clearly rejected the existing spiritualities based upon the traditional Indian religious thinking, which include ways connected with 'ascetic', *yuga* and 'knowledge'. Because Guru Nanak Devji's rejection of the existing spiritualities and proposing an alternate spirituality, was based upon his personal religious experiences, which one can only follow by obeying His will, according to His order (*Hukami*), we can say his 'spirituality' or 'Sikh spirituality' is in real sense was/is 'counter spirituality'.

Guru Nanak Devji did not stop by just raising a question and answering the same as we have seen above. He has also spelled out his spirituality throughout his hymns and other Gurus have followed him. But Guru Nanak Devji, based upon his experiences, also formulated five stages of spiritual development, which he has stated in *Japuji Sahib* (verses 35-8). *Dharam Khand* (the realm of duty), namely *Gyan Khand* (the realm of knowledge), *Saram Khand* (the realm of the bliss), *Karam Khand* (the realm of grace) and *Sachi Khand* (the realm of truth).

(a) *Dharam Khand* is the first stage, in which all human beings are placed equally on this earth (world) to do their job or duties. Here the stress is on moral or ethical duties of human beings, on the performance of which depends moving into the next stage.
(b) *Gyan Khand* is the second stage, in which a human being tries to gain the knowledge of God and this Universe. In this stage, a person is supposed to know about his/her limitations, as against the vastness of this Universe and its Creator. This knowledge

helps one in dissolution of one's ego or self-centeredness, which allows one to treat all equally, without any prejudices. This positive experience of God and Universe on the one side adds knowledge about one self, on the other side helps the person to enter into the next stage of his/her spiritual journey.

(c) *Saram Khand* is the third stage, in which the human being experiences the development of his inner self's facilities and sensibilities. It adds to the mind and intellect aesthetic healthy and also refines the physical sense in such a way, that the human being starts experiencing the glorious immanence of Divine Reality in this Universe. This experience of Divine presence, helps the person to enter into the next stage of life journey.

(d) *Karam Khand* is the fourth stage, in which the human being receives the grace of God. It is receiving the Divine grace, which assures the human being, the fulfilment of his/her search of journey and it also gives him/her strength to enter into the next and final stage of his spiritual journey.

(e) *Sach Khand* is the fifth and final stage of human spiritual journey and according to Guru Nanak, it is here in this realm, where the Formless, the eternal Being, God Himself lives. Here at this stage the human being comes in complete communion with the Formless or becomes one with Him and with the realities of this Universe. It is here the human being meets face to face infinity and transcendental aspects of the Ultimate Reality (Ik Omkar).[10]

About the Sikh spiritual or mystical journey, which includes all the above five stages, Nikky-Guninder Kaur Singh says

it 'is not a journey away from our world. Rather, it is grounded in and this earth. It is here in our everyday existence that we develop our moral, intellectual, aesthetic and spiritual capacities and experience and ultimate Reality. The journey begins and ends in love and her beings. . . . Sikh mysticism is based on drawing the Ultimate into the human situation. Thus we live in the truest sense, living as life would be in *Sach Khand*, the Realm of Truth.[11]

As mentioned earlier, in this chapter the discussion is limited to the views of the founder Guru Nanak on the theme of 'Sikh spirituality', but it must be also mentioned that this theme was further developed by the other nine Gurus too. During this development of thoughts on 'spirituality', based upon the experience of various Gurus, a number of expressions came in use, which are presently also used by the Sikh believers. A brief reference to some of these expressions may further help in understanding the nature of 'Sikh sprituality'. One of the most important expressions which Guru Nanak Devji used was *Sahaj*. *Sahaj* according to the *Sikh Encyclopaedia*, 'applied to human beings, implies practice of voluntary and gradual discipline of the body and mind, as against compulsory asceticism or modification which is generally the practice of the *Yogis*'. Guru Nanak Devji says: 'To see Nature, to hear Gurbani, to utter the Holy name, thus the treasure of honour is obtained through *Sahaj* contemplation.'[12]

The other important expression which has been used by the later Gurus to describe the 'life' or 'spritual life' of a Sikh are: *deg-tegh*, *miri-piri* and *sant-sipahi* (saint-soldier). The expressions *deg-tegh* (*deg* means a big cooking pot and *tegh* means word). This expression in combination of *deg-tegh* was used to express the idea of 'service' and 'protection' and it refers to 'worldly' and 'spititual' powers. These expressions were used in the present sense more by the Sikh Guru Hargobindji and tenth Guru Gobind Singhji. But it was Guru Hargobindji, who for the first time wore two swords, one to denote his spiritual power and the other was used by Guru Gobind Singh also.[13] S.S. Narang has summarized the meaning of *miri-piri* as used in the Sikh traditions, which we are quoting below, because it will serve as a good conclusion of our discussion on Sikh spirituality.

> *Miri* is the symbol of worldly activities and virtues of political power, courage and bravery. . . . *Piri* represents the spiritual aspects of life and virtues such as love, compassion, humility and self-sacrifice, etc. *Miri*, represents the physical material and worldly aspects of life where *piri* signifies the subtle and spiritual aspects of life. . . . *Miri-piri* is a special kind of co-related balance between the material pursuits and spiritual pursuits, an equipoise of earth-awareness and God consciousness; it represents the Sikh ideal of *bhakti* and *shakti*-saint-soldier . . . a balanced development of body and spirit. It is like the two wings of a flying bird. It is a skillful cosmic way—while fully engages in life to remain disengaged. Its balanced state (*shaj avastha*) is the ideal combination of *miri-piri*.[14]

NOTES

1. Kirpal Singh (ed.), *Janam Saki Parampara* (Punjabi), Patiala, 1969, pp. 17-23.
2. Ibid., pp. 35, 36.
3. Ibid., pp. 125-9.
4. James Massey, *The Doctrine of Ultimate Reality in Sikh Religion: A Study of Guru Nanak's Hymns in the Adi Granth*, Delhi, 1991, rpt. 2010, pp. 5-7.
5. Gurmukh Nihal Singh (ed.), *Guru Nanak, His Life, Time and Teachings*, Delhi, 1981, pp. 29-34. (These pages should be referred for a detail discussion and for translation of Guru Nanak's hymns quoted here concerning 'Religion in Decline' in Guru Nanak's time.) See also *SGGS*, p. 306.
6. Massey, op. cit., p. 144.
7. *SGGS*, p. 722.
8. Ibid., p. 1.
9. Ibid.
10. Nikky-Guninder Kaur Singh (tr. & intro.), *The Name of my . . . Beloved, Verses of the Sikh Gurus*, San Francisco, 1995, pp. 13-15.
11. Ibid., p. 15.
12. Ramesh Chander Dogra and Gobind Mansukhani, *Encyclopaedia of Sikh Religion and Culture*, Delhi, 1995, p. 403.
13. Ibid., pp. 122, 123.
14. See in Kharak Singh (ed.), *Current Thoughts on Sikhism*, Chandigarh, 1996, pp. 235-6.

7

Charity

INTRODUCTORY REMARKS

Most English dictionaries agree while listing the meaning of the term charity, 'alms giving or performing other benevolent actions of any sort for the needy with no expectations of material reward'.[1] in general this meaning of the term 'charity' is correct, but there is also a special meaning which *Chambers English Dictionary* has listed as 'universal love'.[2] Here in these meanings of the term charity the most important meanings to note are almsgiving and love.

Almsgiving in a number of Indian religious tradition, is linked with the concept of *pun-dan*, which of course includes the concern for others also, but in return some kind of reward is also expected and either spiritual or worldly.[3] But where the concept of universal love is concerned, here return reward plays a minimum role. Therefore, while looking into the whole concept of charity in Sikh religion, we will try to look in which meaning the concept of charity is understood and practised by the followers of Sikh religion.

It will not be possible to go into details of all the aspects of charity in Sikh religion, but still an attempt is being made here to present as clearly as possible the meaning of this concept by referring to the most important aspects of the same and also by referring to the most important sources of Sikh religion. For the sake of convenience we have divided our discussion into the following three subheads:

- Sources,
- Important concepts, and
- Concrete forms.

1. SOURCES

The *Sri Guru Granth Sahib*, the Sikh scripture, is the primary source for the Sikh fundamental teachings on various subjects and issues. Besides this basic source, the other main source is the *Sri Dasam Granth Sahib*, the Scripture of the Tenth Guru. After these two sources come the other important secondary sources including the *Vars* (ballads) of Bhai Gurdas, *Rahitnamas*: the code of conduct, *Sikh Rahit Maryada*: the life-rules, and *Janam-sakhis*: which contain the life stories of the Gurus and various other old Sikh writings and traditions. But here in this brief chapter it will not be possible to refer to all these sources, therefore we will be referring only to the main sources, the *Sri Guru Granth Sahib*, *Vars* of Bhai Gurdas and the *Rahitnamas*.

Guru Nanak Devji's teachings about charity is to be found in a number of his writings. But in one of his writings *Var Asa* he has dealt specially with some of the issues which are directly connected with the daily life of a human being. In *Var Asa*, Guru Nanak Devji has laid an emphasis on both the service of God as well as of a fellow human being. In this *Var* he has also explained the true nature of charity as well as the false nature of the same. He has specially laid emphasis on sharing one's earnings with others. A few verses from *Var Asa* are quoted in support of Guru Nanak Devji's views on charity. He says to a human being:

Je loṛahi caṅgā āpaṇā kari puṅnhu nīcū sadāīai.

If you desire your good, O human being,
perform virtuous deeds *kari punnhu* and feel lowly.[4]

Guru Nanak Devji rejects the idea of good works and deeds carried on as mere ritual with an attention to achieving salvation, which includes various charities also. These, according to him are false. According to him:

Lakha nekīā caṅgāīā lakhu punnā paravāṇu.
Lakha tapa upari tīrathā sahaja joga bebāṇa . . .
Nānak matī mithiā karamu sacā nīsāṇu . . .

Numerous of virtues and good actions, numerous of approved charities [punna]. Numerous of penances at holies . . . Nanak. These acts of wisdom are false and true is the mark of grace. . . . [5]

But certainly Guru Nanak Devji has laid stress on sharing one's honest earnings with others. He says in this regard:

Nānak agai so milai jì khate ghāle dei.

Nanak, in the next world, that alone is received,
which one gives from one's earnings and labour.[6]

More clearly about serving others Guru Nanak Devji says in one of his hymns:

Sevā surati sabadi vīcāri.

Meditating on the Name, human being get accustomed to serve *seva* others.[7]

Angad Devji, the second Guru has also stressed on selfless sacrificial service. He says:

Āpu gavā sevā kare tā kichu pae mānu.

A human being shall obtain respect only by sacrifice of self and rendering service [*seva*].[8]

According to Guru Arjan Devji, the fifth Guru, a true devotee of Guru Nanak Devji has to be 'the servant of servants [*das dasan*]'.[9]

The *Vars* written by Bhai Gurdas is considered to be the best commentary on the writings of the Gurus.[10] The same is true with his interpretation of the concept of charity. Some of the verses are listed below as examples. In *Var* 12 he says:

> I sacrificed myself for a person who wholly does good to others [*paropakar*] feels happy.[11]

In *Var* 14 Bhai Gurdas narrates the basis of a service being rendered by a Sikh believer. He says:

> By making the teachings of Guru part of life. Sikh believers continue to do service [*seva*].[12]

In *Var* 28 he very clearly lays emphasis on the three golden rules of Sikh life by saying:

> A Sikh believer should eat out of hard labour *ghali Khai*, render service [*seva karai*], and follow Guru's teachings [*Gur-upades*].[13]

In *Var* 40, Bhai Gurdas also tells that a true Sikh brings his offering from his earnings to the place of service. Secondly, a Sikh always first offers food to others and afterwards whatever is left over he/she eats.[14] Harjot Oberoi has summarized the teachings of Bhai Gurdas on the daily life of a Sikh as follows:

> Bhai Gurdas advised the faithful to be humble, courteous and charitable, to eat, speak and sleep in moderation, and by doing so transcend the human ego. Unrestrained human energies and chaotic living can lead to sorrow and pain. The ideal way to overcome these afflictions and lead a harmonious life is to practice the precepts of the Gurus.[15]

With the passing of time the Sikhs have also developed life-rules or code of conduct to govern their daily life. The life-rules are known as *Rahitnamas* and *Sikh Rahit Maryada*. About the origin of these rules it is believed that the tenth Guru Gobind Singh gave oral instructions to a number of Sikh believers, the Khalsa, from time to time, which later on have taken the form of writings.[16] The most well-known *Rahitnamas* are those of Bhai Daya Singh, Bhai Chaupa Singh, Bhai Nand Lal and Bhai Desa Singh.

Bhai Nand Lal has dealt in detail in his *Rahitnamas* about service rendered to others, which in a real sense is service to Gurus.[17] According to Bhai Nand Lal, one day he had a meeting with Guru Gobind Singhji and during the conversation, Guruji told him that a Sikh should offer service to the 'hungry and naked' and this he should do joyfully. To offer service is one of the most important duties of a Sikh. Guruji further made it clear that while offering service, a Sikh should not make a difference between upper caste or lower caste, a religious person or non-religious person. He said that everyone should be considered *gurubhai*, i.e. a brother or sister in Guru or the purpose of service.[18]

Bhai Chaupa Singh in his *Rahitnama* says:

> *Guru ka Shikh Garib di rasana, Guru ka Golak jane*[19]

> A disciple of Guru should take care of the poor, considering the poor as Guru's charity box.

Bhai Desa Singh in his *Rahitnama* has stressed upon giving one-tenth, i.e. *daswand.* He says:

> A Sikh should give one-tenth of his earnings to religious and charitable causes.[20]

The document named *Sikh Rahit Maryada* adopted by Shiromani Gurdwara Parbandhak Committee (SGPC) at Amritsar in 1983 has affirmed and upheld the principle of service as one of the basic part of Sikh faith.[21]

The above in brief is the survey of the Sikh religious written sources with regard to the teachings of Sikh religion on the concept of charity for which we have seen the above two expressions used are *seva* and *punn*, but with the meaning of 'universal love' or 'selfless love'. Now before moving on to the description of the practical and concrete forms of Sikh service, here a brief reference needs to be made to the following four important concepts, which will make the application aspect of the above teachings more clear: *gurmukh*, *daswand*, *vand chhako* and *langar*.

2. IMPORTANT CONCEPTS

2.1. *Gurmukh*

Gurmukh literally means the 'mouth of the Guru' and its implied meaning is 'a person who leads a life according to Guruji's words or instructions'.[22] But besides these general meanings, the *gurmukh* has three levels of deeper meanings also, which actually are the basis of Sikh charity or service rendered by different categories of Sikhs. Avtar Singh in his work *Ethics of the Sikh* has discussed in detail the meaning of these three levels of the *gurmukh.*[23] The first level is known as *gurmukh.* According to this category the *gurmukh* follows a set rule for life 'do unto others as they do unto you', which means 'return good for good and evil for evil'. The second level is known as *gurmukhtar,* according to which a person turned his/her back to evils and instead of that tried to follow the Gurus teachings. If anybody will do good to a *gurmukhtar,* he/she will not forget that and would always try to show gratitude for the same. He will always try to offer help to the needy. The third level is known as *gurmukhtar,* which is applied to a person who treats all equally while rendering service. For *gurmukhtar* there is no difference between a friend and an enemy.

2.2. *Daswand*

Daswand means 'one-tenth' and it is the tenth Guru Gobind Singh, who commanded his disciples, the Sikhs, to contribute *daswand* of his/her earnings to organize Sikh charities for religious purposes.[24] The earlier references have already been made to *Rahitnama,* particularly of Bhai Desa Singh, according to which *daswand* is compulsory for religious and charitable causes. In a way *daswand* is the main source of charitable works in Sikh religion.

2.3. *Vand Chhako*

In Sikh religion, there are three golden rules which are supposed to govern the life of a Sikh. These are: *kirat karo, vand chhako* and *nam japo.* The first, *kirat karo* means that one should earn one's livelihood by honest creative labour; the second, *vand chhako,* means to share the fruits of one's labour with others and third, *nam japo,* means to meditate on God's name.[25] Here we are not concerned with all the three rules, though all three are interconnected, but our subject 'charity' is directly related to the second rule namely *vand chhako.* Here in this rule emphasis in Sikh teaching is on 'selfless services' to others. According to this rule one who will think of doing good to others, for him/her one of the first steps is to share with others one's earnings. This is quite different from giving a *dan* or almsgiving. In the process of *dan* one is always a 'beggar, and the other is a giver, one is a dependent 'slave', and the other is a 'master', but *vand chhakana* lays emphasis on equality.[26] This principle makes the Sikh charity concept most positive in sense and meaning.

2.4. *Langar*

In a way the above three interrelated concepts of Sikh religion are summed up in the last and fourth concept, which is more practical in nature, namely *langar*, i.e. free kitchen. Sikh giving in the form of *daswand*, supports *langar*. It is also an open expression of *vand chhako*. Therefore *daswand*, *vand chhako* and *langar* are the practical expressions of the life of a *gurmukh*. These depend on the charity practices of Sikh religion. Along with *langar*, the other two important concepts connected are *pangat* which means a group of people sitting in a row, and *deg* and *tegh*, which mean a big cooking pot and a sword.

To begin with, *langar* was started by the first Guru Nanak Devji as a token of human brotherhood or sisterhood and to help those who are in need. Angad Devji, the second Guru continued to follow this practice, but the third Guru Amar Dasji institutionalized the same. The tenth Guru Gobind Singhji even ordered his followers to start or practise at a personal level, so that nobody may go hungry. The sharing of food in a *langar* always is taken while sitting in a *pangat*. Guru Amar Dasji even ordered his followers that they first serve food to the congregation and then should assemble for prayers. He said: *Pahle pangat piche sangat*, i.e. 'first sitting and eating together and then take part in the fellowship'. *Pangat* today has become a synonym for *langar*. At present this practice has been made a part of Sikh service in every Sikh temple or gurdwara. *Langar* is the direct corporate responsibility of the Sikh community as a whole. It does not depend on givings of outsiders or others.

Langar besides being the practical expression of social equality and integration, is

> a place of training voluntary service and the practice of philanthropy and equality. Service is involved in the collection of fuel and rations, cutting vegetables, cooking of food, distribution of meals, serving of drinking water, washing of utensils and dishes, and the cleaning of dining halls. It is a practical demonstration of hospitality and love of human beings.[27]

3. CONCRETE FORMS

Of course, Sikhs are known for both corporate as well as individual service to the community as a whole. The examples of an individual Sikh service, we find in the form of *pingalwara* which means a home for the crippled. *Pingalwara* was started by a Sikh named Bhagat Puran Singh, and was established in Amritsar in August 1947. To begin with, he did some service to the community, particularly to destitutes and the sick who needed help. Later on with the help of public contributions, he built a three-storey building for 250 patients. Of course, in this effort, support was offered by the Sikh Shiromani Gurdwara Prabandhak Committee and the Punjab government also.[28] Today, besides its headquarters in Amritsar, it has also two branches in two other places in the Punjab, one at Goindwal and another at village Pandori Waraich with the capacity of housing 70-80 inmates in each. This service is also being expanded to other cities such as Jallandhar.

Different kinds of charity work in a more organized form have been carried on by one of the main Sikh bodies named Chief Khalsa Diwan, which was founded in 1902 with a number of objectives, which also included, 'the uplift of the Sikhs in all spheres, spiritual, social, moral and economic', and 'the removal of illiteracy and spread of education amongst all irrespective of caste and creed'.[29]

In the area of service and charity, Chief Khalsa Diwan started the following institutions: Central Khalsa Orphanage, Amritsar, in 1904, Khalsa Dastkari School for Girls, Amritsar, in 1913; Ashram for the Blind, in 1934; Homeo Hospital, Amritsar, in 1942 for free treatment, and Khalsa Hospital, Tarn Taran.

At present a number of educational and other institutions are being run by the Sikh community all over the country as an expression of their faith, in order to carry on the teachings and commands of their Gurus.

NOTES

1. *Webster's Encyclopedic Unabridged Dictionary of the English Language*, New York, 1983, p. 248.
2. *Chambers English Dictionary*, Delhi, 1990 (rpt.), p. 240.
3. Bhai Kahan Singh, *Mahan Kosh: Encyclopaedia of Sikh Literature* (in Punjabi), Patiala 1981, p. 776.
4. *Adi Sri Guru Granth Sahib* (in Punjabi), Sri Damadami Bir, Pana 1430, Amritsar, n.d., p. 465 (in the subsequent references its abbreviation is only used as *AG*).
5. *SGGS*, p. 466.
6. Ibid., p. 472.
7. Ibid., p. 1343.
8. Ibid., p. 474.
9. Ibid., p. 9.
10. Pandit Narain Singhji Giani (ed.), *41 Varan Bhai Gurdasji* (in Punjabi), Amritsar, 1983, p. 2 (in the case of Bhai Gurdas's *Varan* only *Vars* number and the verse are listed in the subsequent references).
11. *Var* 12: 5: 6.
12. *Var* 14: 17: 7.
13. *Var* 28: 6: 44.
14. *Var* 40: 11: 5-8.
15. Harjot Oberoi, *The Construction of Religious Boundaries: Culture, Identity and Diversity in the Sikh Tradition*, Delhi, 1994, pp. 50-1.
16. Gobind Singh Mansukhani, *The Quintessence of Sikhism*, Amritsar, n.d. p. 215.
17. Piara Singh Padam, *Rahitname* (in Punjabi), Amritsar, 1991, p. 55.
18. Ibid., p 64.
19. Ibid., p. 85.
20. Ibid., p. 147. Also see Gobind Singh Mansukhani, op. cit., p. 216.
21. *Sikh Rahit Maryada* (in Punjabi), Amritsar, 1993, p. 23.

22. Ramesh Chander Dogra and Gobind Singh Mansukhani, *Encyclopaedia of Sikh Religion and Culture*, Delhi 1985, p. 188.
23. Avtar Singh, *Ethics of the Sikhs*, Patiala, 1983, pp. 188-95.
24. Dogra and Mansukhani, op. cit., p. 120. Also see Mansukhani, op. cit., p. 212.
25. *Studies in Sikhism and Comparative Religion*, Delhi, vol. VI, October 1987, nos. 2, p. 34 and vol. VII, April-October 1988, nos. 1 & 2, p. 19.
26. Piara Singh Padam, op. cit., p. 12.
27. Dogra and Mansukhani, op. cit., pp. 122-3, 284-5, 353.
28. Ibid., p. 371.
29. Ganda Singh (ed.), 'The Singh Sabha and Other Socio-Religious Movements in the Punjab 1850-1925', *The Punjab Past and Present*, vol. VII, part I, April 1971, sr. no. 13, Patiala, pp. 66-7.

8

Suffering and Death

1. INTRODUCTORY REMARKS

'Suffering and Death' is one of the main themes which runs throughout the text of the Sikh scripture, yet very little has been written on this theme. Studies of Sikhism and Sikh Gurus such as those by Greenless Duncan, Mark Juergensmeyer and N. Gerald Barrier, and L.M. Joshi have only a few pages on this theme.[1] Our main sources apart from the *Sri Guru Granth Sahib,* are the essays by Gurbachen Singh Talib on 'A Perspective on Suffering',[2] by Wazir Singh on 'The Sikh Perspective on Suffering and Death',[3] and Raghubir Singh Tak on 'Social Suffering and Sikhism'.[4] These three essays are helpful for getting to know other views, particularly the views of Sikh scholars on this theme.

This chapter is based primarily on the text of Guru Nanak Devji's hymns found in the *Sri Guru Granth Sahib.*[5] An early incident is also referred from the life of Guru Nanak Devji, which is taken from the *Janamsakhis* (Life Testimonies) of Guru Nanak Devji, translated by W.H. McLeod.[6] The third source referred to is *Sohila*, which is the night prayer of the Sikhs and is also recited at funeral services. This prayer includes five hymns—three by Guru Nanak Devji, one by the fourth Guru Ram Dasji, and one by the fifth Guru Arjan Devji.[7]

To keep this issue manageable, efforts are limited to deal with the given subject by referring to the teaching of the founder Guru of Sikhism, Guru Nanak Devji.

For conveniences' sake, the discussion is divided into two parts, one 'on suffering,' and the other 'on death' and at the end a brief concluding remarks are addresed.

2. ON SUFFERING

To open the subject 'On Suffering' in Sikhism, I would like to begin with an incident from the early life of Guru Nanak Devji. Almost all of the *Janamsakhi* writers have depicted Guru Nanak Devji as being very strange, from his infancy as well as in his youth. This conclusion was drawn because from the very beginning Guru Nanak Devji's behaviour towards his family and to the affairs of this world were very different when compared to the average boy. This was a source of worry to his parents. His parents got him married and he had two sons, but it had no effect on his strange behaviour. At one stage, Guru Nanak Devji stopped talking with others and did not care to eat or drink. The whole family became worried and forced his father, Kalu to call a physician to treat Guru Nanak Devji. A part of what happened afterwards is given below from an English translation by McLeod:

> When the physician grasped his wrist
> Guru Nanak withdrew his arm and, drawing up his feet sat up. 'What are you doing, physician?' he asked. 'I am diagnosing the illness which has disturbed your state of mind,' answered the physician.

Guru Nanak Devji laughed and recited the following *shlokas*:

> They called a physician (to practise his) art,
> to seize (my) wrist and feel (my) pulse.
> The ignorant physician was unaware that the
> pain (is in my heart)!
> Return to your home, physician, and do not
> take my pulse.

> A little help I can give myself, but what medicine can you prescribe?

You can be accounted a master physician only if first
you can diagnose the disease.
Seek that medicine whereby all diseases are driven away.

I was seized with agony and the physician came.
He stood over me and prescribed much medicine.
My body weeps, my spirit cries out, but the
physician is unable to prescribe any treatment.
Return to your home, physician, you know nothing.
The Creator who caused this agony—He, Nanak
is the One who can cure it.

After reciting the above *shlokas*, Guru Nanak Devji sang another *shabad* concerning the physician, in which he stressed both the suffering and the pain he had and about the cure, which was possible. He said

. . . For it is my heart which suffers torment.
. . . Agony is a poisonous plant; the Name of God its cure.
Grind (the Name) on the stone of tranquillity,
(pour it into), the flask of Truth.
Take it daily and your body shall never waste away. . . .

On hearing this *shabad*, the physician told Guru Nanak Devji's father that he should not worry, because Guru Nanak Devji was alright and would in the future help others in their sufferings.[8]

This incident in Guru Nanak Devji's life tells us a number of things about suffering and pain with which Guru Nanak Devji was concerned. To put it briefly, suffering here, according to this incident, is the 'inner suffering'. How does such suffering come about? According to Guru Nanak Devji, the Creator Himself has caused it and only He can cure it. Human beings can receive this cure by repeating God's name and meditating on Him. 'Suffering' (though it is more spiritual in nature), as this incident makes clear, has been the major concern of the founder Guru of Sikhism and therefore it is also the concern of the Sikh religion.

Guru Nanak Devji, in his hymns, has made a number of references to different kinds of suffering. According to him, all suffering came with the created world.[9] Both 'pleasure and pain' (*sukh dukh*) have come through God Himself. But the disciple of

Guru (*Gurmuk*) is not affected with this. Pride (*haumai*) is the root cause of suffering.[10] In a number of his other hymns Guru Nanak says very clearly that it is God who controls both 'pleasure and pain'. For example, in his famous writing *Japu,* Guru Nanak Devji says:

Hukami likhi dukh sukh paiahi.[11]

by His written command they suffer pain and pleasure.

Guru Nanak Devji says the same thing in another hymn, when he says, 'pain and pleasure are in His order (*bhanai*) and will (*rajai*)'.[12] Again in another place he says that pain and pleasure are in the hands of the Lord, the Creator.[13] In a number of other hymns Guru Nanak Devji repeats the same point.[14]

How and why do living beings suffer? Guru Nanak Devji has answered this question in several ways. In some of his hymns, he compares human beings with a bride whose husband has forsaken her; because of this 'separation' the human being (she) suffers.[15] Another reason for suffering and illness in this world, according to Guru Nanak Devji, is lustfulness (*bhog*) and because of it, the world weeps.[16] To be good or bad is also to be responsible for 'pain and pleasure'.[17] Guru Nanak Devji also recognized the fact of war and political greed as a factor responsible for the suffering of people.[18] The pride of human beings is one of the root causes of human suffering.[19] Enjoying worldly pleasures in excess, including sexual pleasures, results in various diseases which ultimately cause pain and suffering before destroying life.[20]

Guru Nanak Devji also speaks about the universality of suffering in many of his hymns.[21] In one hymn Guru Nanak emphatically declared, *Nanak dukhia Sabhu Sansaru* (Guru Nanak Devji, the whole world is suffering). To support this famous thesis of his on 'suffering', he quoted examples from the ancient history of India as well as examples in general from nature which were applicable to everyone in this world. For example, Nanak noted: Lord Inder suffered because of a punishment of the thousands marks of vulva; Ajai wept when he was made to eat the dung which he gave in charity; Lord Rama cried when he was exiled, and when his wife, Sita, and his brother Lakshman, separated from him; Ravana wept when he saw his Kingdom Lanka (Ceylon) destroyed; the Pandavas also cried when they became servants to their conquerors during their exile; the Divine teachers and kings wept when they faced different kinds of agony. Even rich misers cried at the loss of their wealth, pandits mourned the loss of their knowledge, and young women wept at the loss of their husbands. Guru Nanak observed that the whole world was crying in this way because of suffering.[22]

But Guru Nanak Devji does not stop after describing the suffering of this world. He goes on to add in the last line of the above hymn that only faith in His (God) name can enable one to overcome this. Nothing else, such as good deeds or work will help in this matter.[23] In a large number of hymns Guru Nanak Devji has laid stress on the grace of God as the means of salvation from all kinds of suffering.[24] Guru Nanak Devji's advice is to treat both 'pain and peace alike' and in this way a person can stay balanced.[25]

Guru Nanak Devji has summed up four different kinds of suffering and, also, a way out from these in one of his hymns of *Malar Raga*, some verses of which are given below in English as translated by Manmohan Singh:

> Firstly I feel the pain of separation from God.
> and another pain is of the hunger for his meditation.
> Another pain is of the fear of strong attack of death's myrmidon.
> Yet another pain is that infested with disease, my body shall pass away. . . .
> All his pain and disease are dispelled.
> Through The True Name, O Nanak, he is delivered and released.[26]

3. ON DEATH

In Sikhism 'death' has two aspects. One is that human beings are led through this earthly life to their final destiny, that is, to union with God. This aspect of death is positive in nature, because it ends the separation or gulf, and it also means the end of earthly suffering/pain, which one faces deep down within one's self during this earthly life. The other is that human beings are led into coming and going (transmigration) into this earthly life, which means also the multiplication of suffering/pain and the continuation of separation from God. This question of separation is the main burden of Sikh religion. The founder Guruji of Sikhism, Guru Nanak Devji, has raised this question right in the beginning of his most important writing, *Japuji Sahib*, in these words:

Kiv sachara hoiai Kiv Kurai tutai pal,[27]

How can one be righteous and how can the veil of falsehood be torn?

All the teachings of the Sikh Gurus, which are found in the *Sri Guru Granth Sahib*, are given in response to this question. The first aspect of death mentioned above or, to be more correct, the first kind of death, which leads human beings to their final destiny, is the answer to this question, and the second kind of death (or the second aspect) mentioned above is the ongoing veil or separation, which continues to bring human beings into this world of suffering.

The best description of the first kind of 'death' is found in the text of the funeral prayer of Sikhism. As mentioned in the beginning of this paper, this prayer has five hymns—three by Guru Nanak Devji, one by Guru Ram Dasji and one by Guru Arjan Devji. The first hymn of this prayer is by Guru Nanak Devji. The English translation of a few lines, with the original words of this hymn, is given below and helps us in understanding the meaning of death of the first kind:

Sanbati saha likhia, mili kari pavoh telu

The year and day of the wedding is fixed, together you pour oil (at the door).

Dehu sajan asisaria, jio hovai Sahib sio melu

Give me blessings, friends, so that I may meet my Lord.

Ghari ghari eho pahucha, sadre nit pavanni.

This message is sent to every house and such invitations are received everyday.

Sadanhara simriai, Nanak se deh avanni

Meditate on the Sender of Invitation, O Nanak, that day is coming.[28]

These are the last four lines of the first hymn of the above-mentioned prayer. The content of the remaining lines is about the praise (*sohila*) of God, the Creator. Here in the above quoted first line, a number of points need to be noted. According to this line, the day or time is already fixed for everyone to leave this world (other word for death). The term used for death or to leave this world for the next, is *saha*, which is used in the Punjabi language even today for sending invitations to fix the date for a marriage, an occasion for happiness. Both at the time of departure from the parents' house and upon arrival at the house of the parents-in-law, oil is poured at the threshold of the house. In this way a symbol is used in order to show that real death is an occasion for happiness and not a sad event. The second line quoted above further makes the meaning of death clear. The person who is dying or leaving, according to this line, requests his/her friends to bless him/her, that he/she may meet (or have) union with *Sahib* (Lord). This being good news, such meeting/union invitations are sent/should be delivered to all. In the other two hymns of Guru Nanak Devji, which are part of the Sikh funeral service, praise to God is sung/given. The last two hymns of the fourth Guru Ram Das and the fifth Guru Arjan Devji have the same theme. For example, in the last hymn, Guru Arjan Devji says that those persons who 'are absorbed in God's name' (*Han Nami samane*), 'fear of the pain of births and death leaves them' (*dukhu janam maran bhav khanda he*) and 'they are united with the Everlasting God' (*Abinasi purkhu paia parmesaru*).[29]

The second aspect of death or the second kind of death about which Sikh scripture talks is the whole question of coming and going into life again and again. The Sikh religion fully recognizes the doctrine of transmigration. The whole process of life (birth) and death is connected with this doctrine. As mentioned above, the Sikh Guru accepts the reality of a person's separation from God. According to Sikhism, until this separation disappears, human beings continue the captivity of the cycle of life and death known as transmigration. But why? Guru Nanak Devji gives an answer to this question in a number of his hymns.

Though Guru Nanak Devji accepts the fact that both birth and death are under the command of God,[30] still he recognizes the fact that a person is himself/herself responsible basically for his/her captivity to the cycle of transmigration. According to Guru Nanak, the attachment to or love for this world or worldly things is one of the main reasons for it. In one of his hymns he says,

Etu mohi duba sansaru . . .
Etu mohi phiri juni pahi.[31]

The whole world is drowned in the worldly love . . .
Because of this love, human being is born again.

Pride (*hau* or *haumai*) is the basic reason for a person's captivity in the cycle of birth and death. Guru Nanak Devji says in one of his other hymns:

In pride (*hau*) man comes, in pride he departs,
In pride he is born, in pride he dies.[32]

In another instance Guru Nanak Devji says the same thing:

He who dies the death of egoism (*haumai*) continues to come and go again and again.[33]

Guru Nanak Devji also says that the person who does not possess such good qualities such as divine knowledge, meditation and self-control will continue to go round in births and deaths.[34]

How can human beings be released from the captivity of the cycle of birth and death? Again Guru Nanak Devji has answered this question in a number of his hymns. He is very definite that a human being does not have any control over life and death.[35] He also recognized the reality of death, which everyone has to face.[36] At the time of death relatives of the departed may cry and lament, but no one can go with him or her, and all this is false (*jhutha*).[37]

According to Guru Nanak Devji, meditation on the Divine Name is one way to overcome the cycle of death, through the gift of the Name enshrined within one's self received from the True Guru (God).[38] When this happens, according to Guru Nanak Devji, death cannot devour such a person.[39] Guru Nanak Devji has specially stressed the role of the Guru, whom one can attain through true service to Him.[40]

Finally, Guru Nanak Devji has laid special stress on the grace of God, which can make it possible for a person to get out of captivity of the cycle of birth and death, and have final union with God.[41]

4. CONCLUDING REMARKS

To sum up the whole discussion on 'Suffering and Death' in Sikhism, it can be said that both 'suffering' as well as 'death' are universal in nature. Everyone in this world has some sort of suffering and, also, everyone faces the challenge of 'death'. One of the root cause of both suffering and death is pride (*haumai*). The way out from captivity to these is by the grace of the Guru (God).

NOTES

1. Duncan Greenless, *The Gospel of the Guru Granth Sahib,* Calcutta, 1975, pp. 71-5, Mark Juergensmeyer and N. Gerald Barrier (eds.), *Sikh Studies: Comparative Perspectives on a Changing Tradition,* Berkeley, 1979, pp. 84-6, and L.M. Joshi (ed.), *Sikhism,* Patiala, 1980, pp. 79-81.
2. Gurbachen Singh Talib, *Guru Nanak: His Personality and Vision,* Delhi, 1969, pp. 227-45.
3. In *The Problem of Death and Suffering in Indian Religions,* ed. Clarence O. McMullen, Delhi, 1983, pp. 126-38.
4. Ibid., pp. 139-56.
5. *Hymns of Guru Nanak,* tr. S. Manmohan Singh, Patiala, 1972.
6. W.H. Mcleod (ed.), *The 840 Janam-Sakhi,* Amritsar, 1980.
7. *Sacred Nitnam,* tr. Harbans Singh Doabia, Amritsar, 1985, rpt., pp. 262-73.
8. McLeod, op. cit., pp. 16-18.
9. *SGGS*, p. 1035.
10. Ibid., p. 1038 (11), p. 1.
11. Ibid., p. 1.
12. Ibid., p. 223.
13. Ibid., p. 352.
14. Ibid., pp. 354, 418, 1023, etc.
15. Ibid., pp. 58, 243.
16. Ibid., p. 413.
17. Ibid., p. 581.

18. Ibid., p. 722.
19. Ibid., p. 906.
20. Ibid., pp. 139, 1034.
21. Ibid., pp. 767, 1110, 1189.
22. Ibid., pp. 953-4.
23. Ibid., p. 954.
24. Ibid., pp. 59, 349, 1109.
25. Ibid., p. 945.
26. *Hymns of Guru Nanak*, pp. 864-5.
27. *AG*, p. 1.
28. Ibid., p. 12.
29. *Sacred Nitnam*, pp. 270-1.
30. *SGGS*, p. 472.
31. Ibid., p. 356.
32. Ibid., p. 466.
33. Ibid., p. 1009.
34. Ibid., pp. 75, 905.
35. Ibid., p. 7.
36. Ibid., p. 24.
37. Ibid., pp. 39, 75.
38. Ibid., pp. 58, 143, 422, 504, 904.
39. Ibid., p. 945.
40. Ibid., p. 19.
41. Ibid., pp. 2, 148, 153, 356, 433, 599.

Part Four

INTERFAITH DIALOGUE

9

Guru Nanak Devji and Interfaith Dialogue

1. INTRODUCTORY REMARKS

The discussion in this chapter is centred around the teachings of Guru Nanak Devji in relation to the whole issue of 'Interfaith Dialogue' in India because it is one of the ways to live in a multi- or pluralistic religious context, such as that prevailing in a country like India. In fact, in some form it always goes on in our various life situations, everyday as well. About the meaning of Interfaith Dialogue, Dr Wesley Ariarajah says:

> At the level of theology, dialogue affirms that this world is God's world. He made it. He remakes it. He is involved in its total history. . . . All religious communities are on a pilgrimage . . . its emphasis is not on religions or systems or ideas, its emphasis falls on people. It says that people are not simply objects for conversions. . . . It is an attempt to understand them as partners with us in a pilgrimage.[1]

Now those of us who have read the life of Guru Nanak Devji as narrated by various authors of the *Janamsakhis*, and his teachings, contained in the hymns in *Sri Guru Granth Sahibji*, will agree with me that Guru Nanak Devji's whole life and teachings are the best example of Interfaith Dialogue. His model can help us in dealing with the present most difficult context of our country. It will not be possible to deal in detail Guru Nanak Devji's life experiences and teachings concerning our subject in this brief chapter, but still an attempt is being made to state a few main points in order to initiate our discussion under the following sub-themes:

- Dialogue in Action,
- Theological Basis, and
- Treatment to other Faiths and Ideologies.

2. DIALOGUE IN ACTION

As mentioned earlier, Guru Nanak Devji's whole life was a part of the process of Interfaith Dialogue and this I call 'dialogue in action'. In this process of Interfaith Dialogue, one basic principle which one has to follow is that one has to presuppose that the Ultimate Truth is part of everyone's faith, and no one can claim a monopoly over the Ultimate Truth. So in the process of dialogue, one can learn about the Ultimate Truth from others and also one can offer constructive criticism about the views of others. But mutual respect towards one another is a demand upon those who get involved in the process of dialogue. But this does not mean that we get lead to syncretism. These principles of Interfaith Dialogue we find functioning in Guru Nanak Devji's way of life. A few examples from Guruji's life will clear this point.

The first example I want to write is Guru Nanak Devji's dialogue with a Pandit. The theme of this *Sakhi* connected with the early life of Guruji is the real nature of study or learning. According to this *Sakhi,* the Pandit was a master in his subject, according to our worldly standard. But young Guruji was not interested in that kind of learning. During the dialogue process, he makes his point clear, part of which, according to the *B40 Janamsakhi*, is as follows, which he said to the Pandit:

> Let your ink be made by burning (your) world affections, let inner love be your pen, and make (your) mind the scribe. And what is written? The Name of God is written! His praises are written, and by the writing thereof all evil is wiped away.[2]

The second incident of Guru Nanak Devji's life which I want to refer to is well known. The editor of *Puratan Janamsakhi* has named this incident *Vehin Parves*. According to this *Sakhi*, after his spiritual experience for some days Guruji kept quiet, but then finally one day he declared the essence of his new experiences in these words:

Jo na Koi hindu hai
Na ko musalaman[3]

There is neither Hindu nor Muslim.

Those of us who have read this *Sakhi* know how a controversy in the form of dialogue took place on Guru's declaration and which later on ended in the mosque and Guruji helped Daulat Khan's qazi to understand the real meaning of *namaz* (prayer). During this dialogue in the form of a *shloka*, Guruji explained the real meaning of Muslim prayer in these words:

Make mercy your mosque, faith your prayer-mat,
And righteousness your Quran.
Make humility your circumcision, uprightness your fasting, and so you will be a (true) Muslim.[4]

Again as it is a well-known fact that Guru Nanak Devji's major part of the life was spent on travels known as *udasi*. It is during these *udasis* that one finds in the real sense 'dialogue in action'. During these travels Guruji visited all the main religious places of major religions of his time, i.e. Hinduism, Buddhism, Islam, Jainism, etc. His visits were not only limited to our own country's four directions, north, south, west and east, he even went to the south up to Sri Lanka and on the other up to the Middle East. It was these visits and travels when Guruji not only offered constructive criticism to various rituals and practices of other faiths, but these also deepened and enriched his religious experience, which later, one can see in the contents of his hymns, in the form of using different divine names and languages. Guruji did not directly attack any religion and did not make an attempt to convert anybody, instead he always tried to strengthen other's faith as part of one's own religion. Here two such well-known examples are cited in support of this argument.

For example, during his visit to Hardwar (for detailed reference see chapter 6), when he saw people throwing water toward the sun in order to send it to their dead forefathers, instead of arguing and correcting people's folly, he started throwing water toward his fields in Punjab. When people questioned him about his action, during the dialogue he answered and pointed to them:

> 'My friends', said Baba (Nanak)Ji,
> 'If water will not reach my field (from here) then how can it reach your forefathers? . . .[5]

Take for example another incident which took place during Guruji's visit to Mecca. When Guruji slept, keeping his feet toward holy place and on questioning by a Muslim priest, he replied:

> *Jit val Khudai ate Kaba nahin,*
> *Tetu vali nerai pair ghasiti kari cadu.*
>
> Whichever direction you think God and Kaba is not, you may drag my feet toward that direction.[6]

The size of this chapter will not permit me here to quote more examples to show how Guru Nanak's whole life was a model of interfaith dialogue, therefore we now move to the next section.

THEOLOGICAL BASIS

While giving the meaning of interfaith dialogue (which has been already referred in the Introductory remarks) Dr. Ariarajah said, 'At the level of theology, dialogue affirms that this world is God's world. He made it. . . .' This fact is equally true in Guru Nanak Devji's teachings about the Creator and creation (see chapter 5). Therefore here I am referring to only a few verses of Guru's one of the hymns on creation. This hymn is found in *Maru Raga* (*SGGS*, p. 1035). The following verses in English translation will serve our purpose.

> There was neither earth nor sky;
> (Only) the infinite (Beings) will was there . . .

when he willed (*bhana*), He made the world;
and without support stretched out the vast expanse . . .
He made the creation and sees it;
And his Order ran through the Universe. . . .[7]

There are a number of important points which one needs to note in the doctrine of creation in the hymns of Guru Nanak Devji, which needs to be explained, underlined, and reiterated for the benefit of the present time. There is firstly the assertion that God has created this universe out of nothing and this He did according to His will (*bhana*). Creation, according to Guru Nanakji is the work of a sovereign God. We are, because God is. With this truth, two things become clear—one is that without God either human beings or this cosmos would be inconceivable. Second, all of us are accountable to a higher authority, meaning God. This means the way we as human beings exercise our stewardship over creation and the manner in which we treat each other, has ultimate consequences which we cannot escape from.

Guru Nanak.Devji's doctrine of creation and human being also reveals another important point for us—that we all have been created by One Creator. We, all men and women, are his creation and therefore are equal before Him. We all are members of one family. It also implies that both in our situation, the oppressors and the oppressed are of the same species. Human life therefore is to be pursued not selfishly, but in a cooperative way, as a human venture.

3.1. *Treatment to Other Faiths and Ideologies*

Already references has been made to Guru Nanak Devji's treatment to other faiths. Here without spelling out I am quoting below one of Guru Nanak Devji's other hymns, which tells us how he treated all faiths equally. This hymn which I have quoted earlier also is actually part of *Ramkali ki Var* which gave a very vivid picture of Guruji's treatment to other faiths and ideologies. Here I am reproducing the English translation as rendered by late S. Manmohan Singh with the original text:

Hindū kai ghari hindū āvai. Sūtu janeū paṛi gali pāvai.
Sūtu pāi kare buriāī. Nātā dhotā thāi na pāī.
Muslamānu kare vadaāī. Viṇu gura pīrai ko thāi na pāī.
Rāhu dasāi othai ko jāī. Karaṇī bājhu bhiṣti na pāī.
Jogī kai ghari jugti dasāī. Titu kārṇī kani mundrā pāī.
Mundrā pāi phirai sansāri. Jithai kithai sirjṇahāru.
Jete jia tete vātāū. Cīrī āī dila na kāū.
Ethai jāṇai su jāe sinnāṇai. Horu phakaṛu Hindū Musalmānai.
Sabhanā kā dari lekhā hoi. Karaṇī bājhahu tarai na koi.
Sacu sacu vakhāṇai koi. Nānak agai pucha na hoi.

The Hindu comes to the house of the Hindu
Chanting the sermon, he puts on the yarn sacred thread on the boy's neck.
Putting on the tread, he commits sins.
For his ablutions and washings he is approved not.
The Muslim praises his faith.
Without the Guru and the Divine teacher, none is accepted.
Even when the way is pointed out rare is the one who reaches there.
Without good deeds, heaven is attained not.
One goes to the Yogi's monastery to ask the way to God.
For that purpose, he puts rings in his ears.
With earrings on, he wanders about the world.
He realises not, the Creator-Lord is everywhere. As many as are the beings, so many are the travellers.
When the death warrant comes, none can make any delay.
He, who knows the Lord here, recognises Him in that place.
Other, whether Hindus or Muslims are but praters.
All mortals' accounts are taken in the Lord's court and none is saved without good deeds.
He who utters the Name of the Truest of the true, O Nanak, is not called to account, hereafter.

4. CONCLUDING REMARKS

In conclusion I want to make two points. *One,* that Guru Nanak Devji's life and teachings do not encourage us to have a 'unified culture' or 'mono culture' or even 'cultural nationalism', in India.

Two, Guru Nanak Devji, as we have seen, has recognized the existence of different religions, cultures, ideologies, etc., and he strengthened these through his constructive and positive criticism. The latter is the basic principle of any real authentic Interfaith Dialogue approach, and needs to go on at all level in our pluralistic society on the model, which Guru Nanak Devji offers to followers in such a situation.

NOTES

1. Wesley Ariarajah, *Dialogue*, Singapore, 1980, pp. 12, 13, 15.
2. W.H. Mcleod (ed.), *The B40 Janamsakhi*, Amritsar, 1980, p. 7.
3. Bhai Vir Singhji (ed.), *Puranthan Janam Sakhi Sri Guru Nanak Dev Ji*, Amritsar, 1971, p. 39.
4. *The B40 Janamsakhi*, p. 24.
5. Ibid., p. 85.
6. *Puranthan Janamsakhi*, p. 186.
7. Quoted in ibid., p. 103.

10

Development of 'Inter-Religious Dialogue' in India with Special Reference to Contribution of the Sikhs

The discussion in this chapter is divided into three sections. In section *one*, the historical development is discussed. Section *two* deals with the contribution of Sikhs and in the last section, concluding remarks are given.

1. HISTORICAL DEVELOPMENT: BACKGROUND

1.1. *Beginning Made in India*

In India the 'dialogue' among the followers of various religions is going on in some form since ancient times. This process can be seen influencing the different religious traditions, both positively and negatively even from Rigvedic time. For example, immolation of women on the funeral pyre of her husband originally belonged to non-Vedic people, but through their encounter, the Vedic people accepted this practice.[1] In the same way, the St. Thomas Christians of Kerala in India, through their encounter with the surrounding religious communities, accepted a number of religious rituals and customs, which have now become a part of their religious and liturgical life.[1] We have also seen in the discussion in chapter 9, how Guru Nanak Devji's life (CE 1469-1539) represents in real sense the 'dialogue in action'. But it is also true that in ancient times or during later periods, neither the term 'dialogue' was used, nor conscious organized efforts were made on the line of the present understanding of the inter-religious dialogue.

Inter-religious dialogue in the modem sense, can be traced back possibly to the time of the Mughal emperor Akbar, who ascended the throne on 14 February 1556 and ruled till October 1605. Emperor Akbar was brought up to some extent in the atmosphere of the liberal outlook of his father Humayun and grandfather Babur. He also came into contact from his early youth with Muslim Sufis (mystics) like Mubarak and his sons. Sufis always had liberal views about the Hindu religion, particularly of Vedantic thoughts. With this kind of mystic influence, Akbar developed a very positive interest in other religions.[2]

Akbar, in order to pursue his multi-religious interests, in 1575 constructed a special new building at Fatehpur Sikri called the *Ibadatkhana* (worship place), where he invited scholars and religious leaders to hold religious discussions. His invitees included scholars of different religions—Hindus, Jains, Parsis, Christians and Muslims—from all parts of the country. At one time to the assembled scholars, he said:

> My sole object, oh wise mullas! is to ascertain truth, to find out and disclose the principles of genuine religion, and to trace it to the divine origin: Take care, therefore, that through the influence of your human passions you are not induced to conceal the truth: and say nothing contrary to the Almighty decrees. If you do, you are responsible before God for the consequences of your impiety.[3]

About the nature of dialogue or discussion which took place at *Ibadatkhana*, the historian Al-Badauni says:

> The learned men used to draw the sword of the tongue on the battlefield of mutual contradiction and opposition, and the antagonism of the sects reached such a pitch that they would call one another fools and heretics. The controversies used to pass beyond the differences of Sunni and

Shia, of Hanafi and Shafi, of lawyer and divine, and they would attack the very basis of belief.[4]

A well-known Muslim author of Akbar's time was Abu'l Fazl, who was commissioned by the Emperor to write about his works. Abu'l Fazl wrote the famous book known as *Ain-i-Akbari*. In the preface to *Ain-i-Akbari*, he writes, in order that

hostility towards them (Hindus) might abate and the temporal sword be stayed awhile from the shedding of blood, that discussions within and without be turned into peace and the thornbrake of strife and enmity bloom into a garden of concord. Assemblies for discussion could then be formed and gatherings of science suitably covered.[5]

1.2. *Development of Present Form: Christian Participation*

The history of the inter-religious dialogue in India in the present sense is influenced through the Christian participation as well as by the historical happenings and sources within and outside the country. In the case of the Roman Catholic Church, the major influence came from the Vatican Council II's positive approach in 1965, which the Council had shown towards other religions, including Hinduism, Buddhism and Islam, by saying:

The Catholic Church rejects nothing of what is true and holy in these religions. . . . The Church, therefore, urges her sons to enter with prudence and charity into discussion and collaboration with members of other religions. Let Christians, while witnessing to their own faith and way of life acknowledge, preserve and encourage the spiritual and moral truths found among non-Christians, also their social life and culture.[6]

Prior to Vatican Council II, in India a Roman Catholic convert Brahmabandhab Upadhyay (who came from the Bengali priestly caste and became Christian in February 1891) had sown the seed of inter-religious dialogue by declaring: 'By birth we are Hindus . . . by virtue of our sacramental rebirth, we are Catholics',[7] Upadhyay's approach later in some form was followed by other Catholic scholars, which included P. Johanns, G. Dandoy,

V. Courtouis, R. Antoine, P. Fallon, J. Monchain and Swami Abhishiktananda.[8] There were a number of consultations and seminars among which an All India Seminars were held in Bangalore in 1969; the International Theological Conference on Evangelization, Dialogue and Development in Nagpur in 1971; All India Consultation on Evanglization in Patna in 1971 and finally the General Meeting of the Catholic Bishops Conference in India (CBCI) in 1974 at Calcutta, gave a call to the Church in India to be an pioneer in inter-religious dialogue, because 'it is in the response of Christian faith to God's saving presence in other religious traditions and the expression of the firm hope of their fulfilment in Christ'.[9]

In some way the Christians belonging to various Protestant traditions have a similar history. Because the world body representing major Protestants and Orthodox traditions namely the World Council of Churches has been influencing the inter-religious dialogue in India. But it is also true that in some areas of dialogue, the major contributions were made by the Indian Christians as part of the development of ecumenical and inter-religious dialogue history.

But unlike the Roman Catholic Church in India having one central body, the CBCI, Protestants do not have any central body, except the National Council of Churches in India (NCCI) to which most of the major Protestant churches are affiliated as member churches along with Orthodox tradition. The NCCI has played a similar role like CBCI (though in a limited sense) in encouraging both the member churches as well as the research institutes in the area of inter-religious dialogue. For example, to begin, it was NCCI, which started the present Henry Martyn Institute (HMI) of Islamic Studies in 1930 with one of the specific objectives to study and research Islam with special reference to the Indian context.[10] Again it was NCCI which facilitated the formation of the Christian Institute for the Study of Religion and Society (CISRS) between 1953 and 1957, which later on became one of the main sources of development of the interfaith dialogue in India.[11]

But behind the initiatives of NCCI and the works of various institutes such as CISRS and Henry Martyn Institute, there is quite a history of long-standing concern with dialogue, which goes parallel with the ecumenical history of the Church. However, as it is not possible to deal with this long history of development, only a few highlights are given.

One of the major historical factors behind the development of dialogue is the one which P.D. Devanandan had pointed out in his work on 'Preparation for Dialogue' and 'Christian Concern in Hinduism', the religious revivalism, which begins around the early decades of the nineteenth century, particularly among the followers of Hinduism, Buddhism and Islam. The reason behind this revivalism was the work of missionaries and the various conversion movements. According to P.D. Devanandan, at that time each of these religions started claiming independently that it alone had the answer to the world's problems where Christian religion has failed, but at the same time, the plea was also put forward that the followers of all religions should work for a peaceful co-existence. In this revivalism the followers of every religion also became socially conscious.[12] The various movements such as the Brahmo Samaj and Arya Samaj were the outer manifestations of this renaissance and revivalism.

The above developments forced the Christian missionaries and churches to rethink their approach to other religions and their mission work. A number of national and international conferences and consultations were held. The most well known among which were (a) The World Missionary Conference at Edinburgh 1910 in which semi-liberal views were expressed. Though it was mentioned that Christianity is the absolute, and Jesus Christ fulfils and supersedes all other religions, yet it was suggested that Christianity should be enriched by the treasures of other religions, (b) International Missionary Council of Jerusalem 1928, in which missionary imperialism was condemned and emphasis was laid on paying respect to the sentiments of the people of other religions, and (c) the third important International Missionary Council was held during 1938 at Tambaram, India. For this Council, the famous Dutch theologian Hendrik Kraemer belonging to the neo-Orthodox

School produced a sizeable volume entitled *The Christian Message in a Non-Christian World.* In short the thesis, which this work put forward was that the revelation of God in Jesus Christ was absolute and final.[13]

The above position was questioned by Indian scholars, including G.V. Job, P. Chenchiah, V. Chakkarai, D.M. Devasahayam, S. Jesudason, Eddy Asirvatham and A.N. Sudarisanam, who also brought a sizeable work entitled *Rethinking Christianity in India* in 1938. In this book Chenchiah's article on 'Jesus and Non-Christian Faiths', made their position very clear in the following words:

> In Europe and other Christian countries, Christians see Jesus only. In the unique situation in India which determines the status and influence of Christianity, we see Jesus in the company of other founders of religions or saviours of men—Buddha, Rama, Krishna. Christianity moves and has its being in the midst of life, active religions commanding the homage of millions and claiming, if human testimony counts for anything, to minister and sustain its followers in the struggle of life, giving them the faith to live and courage to die with hope for the future. In India these religions are in numbers and influence such as to compel mutual attention and respect. The life and destiny of Christians has to be studied in this vital context.[14]

By looking very closely at the above opposing views, it is correct to conclude that the conflict between the liberal and neo-Orthodox theologians gave birth to inter-religious dialogue during the second half of the twentieth century.[15]

One outcome of the various ecumenical conferences and council was the formation of the World Council of Churches in 1948, which continues to help and encourage various member churches and councils all over the world, including India, to enter more and more in the process of inter-religious dialogue. Steward E. Brown in his work *Meeting in Faith*[16] has listed and described sixteen of the international and regional consultations which WCC organized between 1969 and 1989. In almost all of these, participants from India, representing Muslim, Hinduism, Buddhism and Christianity have taken part, and these participations have also helped in encouraging the inter-religious dialogue work at the national level in India. The WCC in August 1968 appointed an Indian scholar Stanley J. Samartha as an Associate Secretary in the Department on Study in Mission and Evangelism, with a special responsibility to peruse the study on the Word of God and the Living Faiths of Men. In January 1971, WCC opened a new sub-unit 'Dialogue with Men of Living Faiths and Ideologies', which became a guiding force in the area of inter-religious dialogue including India.[17] This sub-unit later provided 'Guidelines on Dialogue with People of Living Faiths and Ideologies'[18] in 1979, which is now available in its 1990 revised form.

Beside the general role of Christians, which include both the Roman Catholic and Protestant traditions, here two Christian ecumenical institutions needs special mention, namely CISRS, Bangalore and the Christian Institute of Religious Studies (CIRS), Batala, Punjab, because these played a pioneer role in starting a direct process and 'interfaith dialogue' between Sikh-Christians along with other faiths. The CISRS besides promoting and supporting the concern of inter-religious dialogue through its journal and research based publications on dialogue,[19] has also helped in developing and establishing the work of dialogue in the country. For example, during December 1962, it organized a dialogue seminar on 'Sikhism and Christianity in the Punjab', which laid the future basis for Sikh-Christian dialogue in the country. The report and presented papers in the seminar were published in *Religion and Society*.[20] About the general basis of this first Sikh-Christian meeting, the former Director of CISRS late Dr M.M. Thomas stated:

> Sikh and Christian scholars are meeting together in this Conference for a conversation on the deepest things of religion, in which they are different. But we meet as men sharing a common humanity. There will no doubt be differences even in the way Sikhism and Christianity define this community of humanness. But I suppose we can all affirm two aspects of this community. First is that we are all faced with the challenge to seek, to know and to respond to ultimate meaning and destiny of our living. Second is that we have a common task of building a society and a nation in which all men realize their dignity as human persons called to love and serve one another.[21]

The next example of an ecumenical institute involved in interfaith dialogue is from north India, namely the CIRS, Batala, Punjab. This institute during the 1970s and 1980s organized a number of seminars, for example, the first major inter-religious seminar from 7-9 December 1973 at Batala on the theme 'Popular Religion in the Punjab To-day'. The purpose of the seminar was to find out what is happening in the religious life of the Punjab at the present time.[22] Participants included from Sikh, Hindu, Muslim, Jain and Christian backgrounds. The other major seminar, the Institute held was on 'The Nature of Guruship' and the purpose of this was to arrive at a fuller and more comprehensive understanding of Guruship according to different religions and religious traditions.[23] The participants included Hindu, Sikh, Christian (both Roman Catholic and Protestant), Muslim, and popular Hindu and Muslim sects like Ahmadiyya and Radhaswami.

1.3. *The Hindus*

As far as the Hindus are concerned, though they have taken part actively whenever they were invited by Christians or others for any inter-religious meetings or seminars, yet their own initiative has been minimum. But it is indeed encouraging to note when during 1994 for the first time in the history of inter-religious dialogue, the 'Indian Council of Philosophical Research' (ICPR), the country's highest institute of philosophy along with Satya Nilayan and the Jesuit Philosophical Research Institute have jointly sponsored a programme on Hindu-Christian dialogue. Fourteen Christian indologists and some Hindu scholars took part in this dialogue meeting and it is also for the first time when Hindu scholars accepted the Christian contribution to Indian philosophy and also agreed with the fact that Indian philosophy does not necessarily mean Hindu philosophy. R. Balasubramanian, Chairman of ICPR said, 'This is the first time the ICPR is sponsoring such a programme as Hindu-Christian dialogue . . . and it intends to continue such a dialogue from different points of view.'[24]

1.4. *The Muslims*

In Section 1.1 references have been made to the Muslim pioneers in the field of inter-religious dialogue, which included Mughal Emperor Akbar, Abu'l Fazl, Sufi Prince Muhammad Dara Shikoh and nineteenth-century's liberal Muslim scholar Sayed Ahmad Khan. To this list of names the more recent supporters' names of inter-religious dialogue form Muslim names can also be added: K.G. Saiyidain (1904-71) and Abid Husayn (d. 1978) of the Islam and the Modern Age Society, and Nisar Ahmed Faruqi of the same society, who is equally committed to the cause of inter-religious dialogue. There are of course more Muslim scholars who support the need of inter-religious dialogue at the present time. To some of them references are made here.

References have already been made to the work of the Indian Institute of Islamic Studies (IIIS) which was founded during 1963 in New Delhi and has been actively involved along with HMI in organizing jointly the inter-religious dialogue seminars right from the years of its foundation. One of the most important seminars hosted by IIIS was in October 1978 on the theme, 'Mosque and Church, their contribution to inter-religious harmony and re-conciliation.' This seminar was jointly organized by IIIS with HMI and the Dialogue Commission of the CBCI. This seminar highlighted the new awareness of the community dimension of dialogue.

Two presentations by well-known Muslim scholars brought out very important points from the Muslim perspectives. Syed Vahiduddin, former Head of the Department of Philosophy, University of Delhi pointed out that the Holy Quran has laid down the basis of inter-religious dialogue. Ziaul Hasan Faruqi of Jamia Millia Islamia, New Delhi in his presentation made a strong plea for the need for religious communities to open up to one another in dialogue and to thoroughly revise traditional attitudes and teachings.[25] There are a number of other efforts at different levels, which either are led by Muslim scholars or through their participation. One such example is the Institute of Objectives Studies (IOS), New Delhi, which deals with common issues faced by the various religious groups specially by minority religions.

2. THE CONTRIBUTION OF THE SIKHS

In the recent years the response to the concern of inter-religious dialogue has come very much from the followers of Sikh religion. Two of the major universities of Punjab have given a lead in this area, namely Punjabi University, Patiala and Guru Nanak Dev University, Amritsar. The Sikh professors and others from these universities have actively responded to the invitations extended to them by various Christian institutions. In the case of Punjabi University, it has a Department of Religious Study, where all religions are taught by professors belonging to different religions. It has organized lectures and seminars on different themes. For example, in March 1985 it organized a three-day seminar on the theme 'Religious Pluralism and Co-Existence'. About 27 scholars belonging to Hinduism, Christianity, Sikhs and Islam participated in this seminar and all through the seminar the need for religious coexistence was felt by everyone.[26] The seminar 'Towards Building a Peaceful Role of Religion' is the other such example, which was later organized by the department of Encyclopedia of Sikhism.

The Guru Nanak Dev University has a department of Guru Nanak Studies, under which it has been organizing inter-religious dialogue meetings and seminars. One of the earliest major seminars was held in March 1973 on the 'Sikh Concept of the Divine' but papers from Christians and Hindus were also invited, which took the form of comparative studies.[27] A major seminar was also organized by Guru Nanak Dev University in March 1991 on the theme 'Co-Existence in Pluralistic Society: Punjab Problems and Prospects'. Here also the participants were from Hindu, Christian, Muslim and Sikh backgrounds.[28]

Besides the above two Punjab universities, there are a number of research institutes, namely the Guru Nanak Foundation, New Delhi; Institute of Sikh Studies, Chandigarh; Gobind Sadan Institute for Advanced Studies in Comparative Religion, New Delhi; and International Institute of Gurmat Studies, Ludhiana. These Institutes are regularly conducting inter-religious dialogue also on different themes. There are some official committees of Sikh temples like Delhi Gurdwara Management Committee, which also often organizes interfaith meetings. For example, the Delhi Committee had a 'National Seminar on Guru Nanak Dev and Composite Indian Culture' on 10 November 1991, to which Hindu, Christian and Muslim scholars were invited to make presentations. In this seminar, I was asked to make a presentation on 'Guru Nanak Devji's Teachings in the Context of Interfaith Dialogue', part of which is used in chapter 9 of this work.

The most recent examples of Sikh contribution to the 'interfaith dialogue' movement in India are the efforts made by the various Sikh educational institutions throughout the country as part of the celebration on the occasion of 300 years of Guruship of *Sri Guru Granth Sahib*. Four such examples are: *first*, an international seminar organized by the Department of Guru Nanak Studies of the Madurai Kamaraj University in South on 17-19 December 2008 on the theme 'Identity and Dialogue in Guru Granth Sahib'; *Second*, the national seminar organized by Sri Guru Gobind Singh College of Commerce (University of Delhi) on 29 January 2009 on the theme 'Sri Guru Granth Sahibji: Apostle of Universal Brotherhood'; *third*, a seminar organized by Mata Sundri College for Women (University of Delhi) on 17 February 2009 on the theme 'Sri Guru Granth Sahib: A Unique Scripture'; and *fourth*, a national seminar organized by the Guru Nanak Study Centre of the Syama Prasad Mukherjee College (University of Delhi) on 26-27 February 2009 on the theme 'Universal Message of Sri Guru Granth Sahib'. The author of this work was invited to make special presentation in all of these four seminars. In fact, chapters 1 and 2 of this work are based on the presentations made by the author in these seminars.

3. CONCLUDING REMARKS

As part of the concluding remarks the following seven points are being offered:

The *first* point which becomes clear is that historically both the Muslim ruler (like Akbar) and the Muslim Sufi (like Dara Shikoh) can be considered in the present sense the earliest pioneers of inter-religious dialogue in India. It was because of their genuine pursuit of the Truth, which is one of the basic principle of many genuine interfaith dialogue.

The *second* point, which becomes clear is that where Christians, both Roman Catholic and various Protestant traditions are concerned, their search for alternative model of 'mission' (through various international and national conferences) and conflict which in this search arose between the two opposing groups of theologians (liberal and neo-Orthodox) gave birth not only to the present ecumenical movement, but it also became responsible for the movement of inter-religious dialogue in the present form.

The *third* point from this chapter is that role of Sikh religion in the whole area of interfaith dialogue is on the increase and actually the various Sikh community supported universities, departments, colleges and research centres are playing a much larger role as compared to other faiths.

The *fourth* point which becomes clear is that it seems the need of the inter-religious dialogue has increased all over the world and as is clear from the case of the increased response of the followers of the major religions of India during the years.

The *fifth* point which becomes clear is that all the living religious traditions contain the best of all others. No one religion can claim the monopoly of the Ultimate Truth. Therefore through inter-religious dialogue efforts should be made to find a common theological platform in dialogue with adherents of all living religious traditions.

The *sixth* point which becomes clear is that the current situation in India created by the ongoing communal and religious conflicts between different religious groups can be dealt only by adopting the inter-religious dialogue approach which it appears is the immediate need of the present time.

Finally, the *seventh* point, which becomes clear is that inter-religious dialogue is an exercise through which the different partners get engaged in order to realize a wider community in which peace and justice will be fully realized, which the followers belonging to different living religious traditions together will be able to build, the lead for which with any doubt can be drawn from the model of interfaith dialogue offered by Guru Nank Devji.

NOTES

1. K.P. Chattopadhyaya, *The Ancient Indian Culture Contacts and Migrations*, Calcutta, 1990, pp. 6, 20.
   Guidelines for Inter-Religious Dialogue (*CBCI Guidelines*), Delhi, October 1989 (2nd rev. edn.), p. 4.
2. Ishwari Prasad, *A Short History of Muslim Rule in India*, Allahabad, p. 284.
3. Quoted in ibid., p. 291.
4. Ibid., p. 291.
5. Quoted in Bikrama Jit Hasrat, *Dara Shikuh: Life and Works*, Delhi, 1982, pp. xxvi, 193.
6. Austin Flannery (ed.), *Vatican Council II: The Conciliary and Post-Counciliary Documents*, Bombay, 1992, p. 654.
7. Kaj, Baago, *Pioneers of Indigenous Christianity*, Bangalore, 1969, p. 36.
8. *CBCI Guidelines*, p. 6.
9. Ibid., p. 7.
10. David T. Lindell, *The Henry Martyn Institute of Islamic Studies, in the Bulletin of Henry Martyn Institute of Islamic Studies* (*HMIIS*), vol. III, nos. 1-4, January-December 1980, pp. 134-5..
11. Richard W. Taylor (ed.), *Religion and Society: The First Twenty-Five Years 1953-1978*, Bangalore, 1982, pp. 1-2.
12. P.D. Devanandan, *Selections from the Books of P.D. Devanandan*, Bangalore, 1983, pp. 3-6.
13. CH. G.S.S. Sreenivasa Rao (ed.), *Interfaith Dialogue and World Community*, Madras, 1991, pp. xvii-xxiii.
14. G.V. Job, *Rethinking Christianity in India*, 1938, Madras, p. 47.
15. Sreenivasa Rao, op. cit., p. xxiii.
16. Stuart E. Brown (compiled), *Meeting in Faith*, Geneva, 1989.
17. Carl F. Hallencreutz, 'A Long-Standing Concern: Dialogue in Ecumenical History 1910-1971', in *Living Faiths and the Ecumenical Movement*, ed. S.J. Samartha, Geneva, 1971, pp. 57-71.
18. *Guidelines on Dialogue with People of Living Faiths and Ideologies* (*WCC Guidelines*) Geneva, 1990.
19. Examples of CISRS, Inter Religious dialogue related publication: (a) P.D. Devanandan, *Preparation for Dialogue*, Bangalore, 1964; (b) Herbert Jai Singh, *My Neighbours (Men of Different Faiths)*, Bangalore, 1st pub. 1994; rpt. 1966; (c) Herbert Jai Singh (ed.), *Inter-Religious Dialogue*, Bangalore, 1967.

20. *Religion and Society*, vol. XI, no. 1, Bangalore, March 1964.
21. Ibid., p. 4.
22. John C.B. Webster (ed.), *Popular Religion in the Punjab Today*, Delhi, 1974, p. 1.
23. Clarence O. McMullen (ed.): *The Nature of Guruship*, Delhi, 1976, p. 1.
24. *National Council of Churches Review*, vol. CXIV, no. 7, August 1994, p. 578.
25. Troll, op. cit., p. 32. (Also read for a summary for Muslim initiative in the field of inter-religious dialogue in Troll, pp. 29-34 up to the period 1980.) Also see for Syed Vahiduddin's contribution in Islam in India: *Studies and Commentaries by Syed Vahiduddin* (ed. Christian W. Troll), vol. III, Delhi, 1986 (particularly chapter on 'The Quran and Inter-Religious Harmony', pp. 137-44).
26. Proceedings of the seminar are published under the title 'Religious Pluralism and Co-Existence', ed. Wazir Singh, Patiala, 1986.
27. Proceedings of the seminar and published under the title *Sikh Concept of the Divine*, ed. Pritam Singh, Amritsar, 1985.
28. Proceedings of the seminar are published under the title *Co-Existence in Pluralistic Society: Punjab Issues and Prophets*, ed. Madanjit Kaur, Amritsar, 1991.

Bibliography

A. PRIMARY WORKS

Adi Sri Guru Granth Sahib (in Punjabi), Sri Damadami Bir, Pana 1430, Amritsar, n.d.

Bhai Vir Singh Ji: *Puratana Janamsakhi Sri Guru Nanak Devji,* Amritsar, 1971.

Cakar Amar Singh (ed.): *Varan Gian Ratnavali Bhai Gurdasji*, Amritsar, n.d.

Giani Pandit Narain Singhji (ed.): *41 Varan Bhai Gurdasji* (in Punjabi), Amritsar, 1983, p. 2 (in the case of Bhai Gurdas's *Varan* only *Vars* number and the verse are listed in the subsequent references).

Jodh Singh and Dharam Singh (trs.): *Sri Dasam Granth Sahib* (text and translation), Patiala, 2006, p. 151. (All the translated English verses of *Sri Dasam Granth Sahib* taken from this translation listed as *SDGS*).

Padam Piara Singh, *Rahitname* (in Punjabi), Amritsar, 1991.

Sikh Rahit Maryada (in Punjabi), Amritsar, 1993.

Sodhi, Teja Singh: *Sri Dasam Guru Chamtkaar* (Punjabi), Amritsar, 2006.

B. TRANSLATIONS

Hymns of Guru Nanak, text with translation by S. Manmohan Singh, Patiala, 1972.

Sacred Nitnam, translated by Harbans Singh Doabia, Singh Brothers, Amritsar, 1985, rpt.

Talib, Gurbachan Singh: *Sri Guru Granth Sahib* (English translation), vols. 1 (1984), 2 (1985), 3 (1987) and 4 (1990), Patiala.

C. REFERENCES/WORKS

Arndt, William F and F. Wilbur Gingrich: *A Greek-English Lexicons of the New Testament and Other Early Christian Literature, Chicago*, 1957, pp. 98-9. *The New Bible Dictionary*, London, 1969.

Chambers English Dictionary, New Delhi, 1990 (rpt.).

Dogra, Ramesh Chander and Dr, Gobind Mansukhani: *Encyclopaedia of Sikh Religion and Culture*, New Delhi, 1995.

S.V., Kahan Singh, *Gurusabada Ratanakara Mahan Kosh*, 'Andaj'.

Shackle, C.: *Guru Nanak Glossary*, London, 1981.

Soanes, Catherine and Angus Stevenson (eds.): *Concise Oxford English Dictionary*, 11th edn., rev., Oxford, 2007.

Teja Singh, *Jap Ji*, Amritsar, 1974.

Webster's Encyclopedic Unabridged Dictionary of The English Language, New York, 1983.

D. OTHER WORKS (ENGLISH AND PUNJABI)

Ariarajah, Wesley, *Dialogue*, Singapore, 1980.

Avtar Singh: *Ethics of the Sikhs*, Patiala, 1983.

Baago, Kaj: *Pioneers of Indigenous Christianity,* Bangalore, 1969.

Banerjee, Anil Chandra: *Guru Nanak and His Times*, Patiala, 1984.

Bhattacharyya, Haridas (ed): *The Cultural Heritageof India*, vol. IV (*The Religions*), Calcutta, 1983.

Brown, Stuart E. (compiled): *Meeting in Faith,* Geneva, 1989.

Chattopadhyaya, K.P.: *The Ancient Indian Culture Contacts and Migrations*, Calcutta, 1990.

Das, Sunil Kumar: '*Sri Caitanya and Guru Nanak*', Calcutta, 1985.

Devanandan, P.D.: *Selections from The Books of P.D, Devanandan*, Bangalore, 1983.

——— *Preparation for Dialogue*, Bangalore, 1964.

Dogara, Ramesh Chandra and Dr. Gobind Singh Mansukhani: *Encyclopaedia of Sikh Religion and Culture*, New Delhi, 1995.

Duncan Greenless: *The Gospel of the Guru-Granth Sahib*, Calcutta, 1975.

Flannery, Austin (ed.): *Vatican Council II: The Conciliar and PostOunciliar Documents*, Bombay, 1992.

Galanter, Marc: *Competing Equalities*, Delhi, 1984.

Ganda Singh (ed.): 'The Singh Sabha and Other Socio-Religious Movements in the Panjab 1850-1925', in *The Panjab Past and Present*, vol. VII, part I, April 1971, sr. no.13, Patiala.

Guidelines for Inter-Religious Dialogue, 2nd rev. edn., New Delhi, October 1989.

Guidelines on Dialogue with People of Living Faiths and Ideologies, Geneva, 1990.

Ganda Singh (ed.): *The Panjab Past and Present* (Parts I and II), Patiala, 1969.

Gupta, Hari Ram: 'A Life-Sketch of Guru Nanak' in *Guru Nanak, His Life, Time and Teachings*, ed. Gurmukh Nihal Singh, New Delhi, 1981.

Gupte, Pranay, *India: The Challenge of Change*, London, 1989.

Gurbachen Singh Talib: *Guru Nanak: His Personality and Vision*, Delhi, 1969.

Gurmukh Nihal Singh (ed.): *Guru Nanak: His Life, Time and Teachings*, New Delhi, 1981.

Hallencreutz, Carl F.: 'A Long-Standing Concern: Dialogue in Ecumenical History 1910-1971', in *Living Faiths and the Ecumenical Movement*, ed. S.J. Samartha, Geneva 1971.

Hasrat, Bikrama Jit: *Dara Shikuh: Life and Works*, New Delhi, 1982.

Identity and Diversity in the Sikh Tradition, Delhi, 1994.

In The Problem of Death and Suffering in Indian Religions, ed. Clarence O. McMullen, Delhi, 1983.

Jafar,.Ghani: *The Sikh Volcano*, Lahore, 1987.

Kapur, Rajiv A.: *Sikh Separation: The Politics of Faith*, London, 1986.

Kaur, Madanjit: *Guru Gobind Singh: Historical and Ideological Perspective*, Chandigarh, 2007.

——— (ed.): *Co-Existence in Pluralistic Society: Punjab Issues and Prospects* (proceedings of the Seminar), Amritsar, 1991.

Kaur, Miss Sahib: *Sikh Thought*, New Delhi, 1994.

Kharak Singh (ed.): *Current Thoughts on Sikhism*, Chandigarh, 1996.

Khosla, B.S.: 'Guru Nanak's Conception of the Origin of the Universe' in *Guru Nanak: A Homage*, ed. K.R. Srinivasa Iyenger, New Delhi, 1973.

Kirpal Singh (ed.): *Janam Saki Parampara* (Punjabi), Patiala, 1969.

Kohli, Surinder Singh: *Philosophy of Guru Nanak*, Chandigarh, 1976.

L.M. Joshi (ed.), *Sikhism*, Patiala, 1980.

Lindell, David T.: 'The Henry Martyn Institute of Islamic Studies', in *The Bulletin of Henry Martyn Institute of Islamic Studies* (HMIIS) vol. III, nos. 1-4, January-December 1980.

Loehlin, C.H.: *The Granth of Guru Gobind Singh and the Khalsa Brotherhood*, Lucknow, 1991

——— *The Sikhs and Their Scriptures*, Lucknow, 1964.

Mansukhani, Gobind Singh: *The Quintessence of Sikhism*, Amritsar, n.d.

Marenco, Edhne: *The Transformation of Sikh Society*, New Delhi, 1976.

Mark Juergensmeyer and N. Gerald Barrier (eds.): *Sikh Studies: Comparative Perspectives on a Changing Tradition*, Berkeley, 1979.

Massey, James (ed.): *Indigenous People, Dalits* (*Dalit Issues in Today's Theological Debate*), Delhi, 1994.

——— *The Doctrine of Ultimate Reality in Sikh Religion: A Study of Guru Nanak's Hymns in the Adi Granth*, New Delhi, 1991, rpt. 2010.

Mcleod, W.H. (ed.): *The B40 Janam Sakhi*, Amritsar, 1980.

——— *The Evolution of the Sikh Community*, Delhi, 1975.

McMullen, Clarence O. (ed.): *The Nature of Guruship*, Delhi 1976.

Narang, A.S.: *Punjab Politics in National Perspective*, New Delhi, 1988.

Narang, S. Kirpal Singh: 'Guru Nanak: Sudharak Jan Krantikari' (in Punjabi), in *Punjabi Dunia*, Guru Nanak Ank (Part One), Patiala, n.d.

National Council of Churches Review, vol. CXIV, no. 7, August, 1994.

Nikky-Guninder Kaur Singh (tr. & intro.): *The Name of my . . . Beloved, Verses of the Sikh Gurus*, San Francisco, 1995.

Oberoi, Harjot: *The Construction of Religious Boundaries: Culture, Identity and Diversity in the Sikh Tradition*, Delhi, 1994.

Phillips, Maurice: *The Teaching of the Vedas*, Delhi, 1976 (rpt.).

Pritam Singh (ed.): *Sikh Concept of the Divine* (proceedings of the Seminar), Amritsar, 1985.

Rao, CH. G.S.S. Sreenivasa (ed.): *Interfaith Dialogue and World Community*, Madras, 1991.

Religion and Society, vol. XI, no. 1, March 1964, Bangalore.

Sher Singh: *Philosophy of Sikhism*, Amritsar, 1986.

Singh, Ganda: 'The Sikh: A Historical Intepretations', in *Religion and Society*, CISRS, vol XI, no.1, March, 1964.

Singh, Herbert Jai: *My Neighbours* (Men of Different Faiths), Bangalore, 1st pub. 1994; rpt. 1996.

——— (ed.): *Inter-Religious Dialogue*, Bangalore, 1967.

Singh, Trilochen: *Guru Nanak: Founder of Sikhism*, Delhi, 1969.

Smart, Ninian: *Doctrine and Argument in Indian Philosophy*, London, 1964.

Studies in Sikhism and Comparative Religion, New Delhi, vol. VI, October 1987, no. 2, and vol. VII, nos. 1 & 2, April-October 1988.

Tandon, Prakash: *Punjabi Saga (1857-1982)*, Delhi, 1988.

Taylor, Richard W. (ed.): *Religion and Society, The First Twenty-Five Years 1953-1978*, Bangalore, 1982.

W.H. Mcleod (ed.): *The B40 Janam-Sakhi,* Amritsar, 1980.

Wazir Singh: 'The Sikh Cosmology', in *Journal of Sikh Studies*, vol VI, no. 2, 2 August 1979.

——— (ed.): *Religious Pluralism and Co-Existence*, Patiala, 1986.

Webster, John C.B. (ed.): *Popular Religion in the Panjab Today*, Delhi, 1974.

———, *The Dalit Christian: A History*, Delhi, 1992.

Index